THE THERAPIST IS THE THERAPY

THE THERAPIST IS THE THERAPY

Effective Psychotherapy II

LOUIS B. FIERMAN, M.D.

JASON ARONSON INC.
Northvale, New Jersey
London

This book was set in 12 pt. New Aster by Alpha Graphics of Pittsfield, New Hampshire.

10 9 8 7 6 5 4 3 2

Library of Congress Cataloging-in-Publication Data

Fierman, Louis B.
The therapist is the therapy : effective psychotherapy II / Louis B. Fierman
p. cm.
Includes bibliographical references and index.
ISBN 0-7657-0047-6 (alk. paper)
1. Psychotherapy. 2. Psychotherapist and patient. 3. Kaiser, Hellmuth. I. Title.
RC480.F53 1997
616.89'14—dc20 96-43253

Printed in the United States of America on acid-free paper. Jason Aronson Inc. offers books and cassettes. For information and catalog write to Jason Aronson Inc., 230 Livingston Street, Northvale, New Jersey 07647-1731. Or visit our website: http://www.aronson.com

To Ella, my wife,

for her unconditional love, encouragement,

and endless reviewing and editing of this manuscript.

CONTENTS

FOREWORD

The turn of the millennium coincides, more or less, with the centenary of modern psychotherapy, one of the defining intellectual movements of the twentieth century. That this movement is under pressure is not news. Or rather, it is common news, as the media are filled with controversy over the trustworthiness of therapists, the efficacy of treatment, and the consequences of external oversight of the enterprise.

Less widely noted is an internal threat to psychotherapy, namely, a peculiar professional amnesia. Save for a simplified version of Freud, psychotherapy seems to have no history. In particular, the treasures of the middle of the century—the work of Murray Bowen, Carl Rogers, and Karen Horney, to name three of many—lie neglected, untaught in residencies and overlooked in the contemporary literature. Certain ideas, to be sure, survive in general form—witness therapists' emphasis on autonomy, empathy, and the "true self"—but they do so without attribution or, perhaps, awareness, and without the complexity that the mid-century innovators brought to their work.

Most grievously forgotten is Hellmuth Kaiser, who, with Horney, carried the torch of Kierkegaard and existentialism here from the Continent. Kaiser, because he came later, was able to integrate into existentialism his observation of interwar years and their translation into the atrocities of Nazism. These social phenomena he attributed in part to the loss of the individual conscience in the delusions of the group.

Like all great psychotherapies, Kaiser's is as much a perspective on the human condition as it is a method of cure. Kaiser begins with a formulation of what he deems the universal symptom, a problem in saying things straightforwardly. Humans use language as much to hide beliefs, values, thoughts, and feelings as to communicate them; they do so out of discomfort with the self—Kierkegaard's existential dread. Behind the universal symptom, Kaiser sees a universal psychopathology, a fear of separateness that leads to desperate fusion, at once a denial of the truths of the self and an interference with the autonomy of the other. The treatment Kaiser brings to bear is an insistent focus past the screen of obfuscation. Kaiser highlights the lack of frankness and simplicity in the patient's words and thereby frees the patient finally to express himself without communicative duplicity. This enterprise has a moral component. As Louis Fierman states in this volume, "The task of the therapist is to behave in such a way as to promote in the patient a feeling of responsibility for his words and deeds."

In this country, Fierman has done yeoman's work to keep Kaiser's work accessible through the publication of the first volume of *Effective Psychotherapy*. Now, thirty-odd years later, Fierman opens a window on his own work as a therapist who follows in Kaiser's footsteps. In particular, Fierman extends Kaiser's method from the individual encounter to group and family treatments and the efforts of the therapeutic hospital ward. Fierman makes a particularly useful distinction when he disaggregates therapies that merely focus on the patient's existential dilemma from those that, like Kaiser's, do so through offering the patient an experience of communicative intimacy with a therapist struggling with these same issues of existential immediacy.

Of course, useful perspectives have been added to psychotherapy since mid-century. Theorists working in recent years have made a convincing case for attachment impulses as primary and not defensive. Feminist psychology, in particular, has shown that autonomy can be an overemphasized ideal when it obliterates connectedness. And the notion of the atheoretical existential encounter seems less plausible today than it once did; all perspectives contain theory. These changes in viewpoint would not surprise Kaiser; he understood that theory is of a given time and place—that therapy must be made on the spot, here and now.

This said, Kaiser's innovations remain remarkably fresh. We still suffer from the universal pathology and still display the universal symptom. No advances in psychotherapy, and no amount of biological reductionism, can obviate the need for individuals to learn to tolerate their boundedness. No change in the conditions of treatment removes the therapist's obligation to allow patients finally to say what they mean.

—Peter D. Kramer, M.D.

ACKNOWLEDGMENTS

The friends and colleagues to whom I am gratefully indebted for reading my ongoing manuscript and/or advising and consulting with me about its content include Leo Berman, M.D., James Green, Ph.D., Fredda Kelly, Ph.D., Howard Kahn, Ph.D., Starrett Kennedy, Ph.D., Anthony LaBruzza, M.D., John Rakusin, Ph.D., and Alan Towbin, Ph.D.

Michael Moskowitz, Ph.D., Publisher, Norma Pomerantz, Director of Author Relations, and Judy Cohen, Senior Production Editor for Jason Aronson Publishers were all most helpful in advising on the publication process.

Ellen McDermott tirelessly provided me with her highly proficient services in completing the many details of preparation necessary for publication.

Gary S. Schulman, computer/word processing consultant, supplied the wizardry that enabled me to perform the required computer tasks.

Dan and Lauren, my son and daughter, are natural-born therapists who taught me the power of communicative intimacy.

And, finally, my heartfelt thanks to the late Hellmuth Kaiser for his teaching and inspiration.

INTRODUCTION

This book is about psychotherapy. It is subtitled *Effective Psychotherapy II* in reference to my earlier book, *Effective Psychotherapy/The Contribution of Hellmuth Kaiser* (Fierman 1965). Hellmuth Kaiser, Ph.D., was a Freudian psychoanalyst who fled Nazi Germany in 1933. After much hardship in France and Israel he was eventually brought by Karl Menninger, M.D., to the Menninger Psychoanalytic Institute, Topeka, Kansas, in 1949 as a training analyst. He became progressively disillusioned with traditional analytic therapy and gradually developed a new approach and technique for treating psychologically ill patients. He abandoned psychoanalytic jargon and format to espouse an interpersonal, face-to-face, nondirective, interactive, communicative-intimacy model of psychotherapy. Although many of his colleagues were attracted to his innovations, the more traditional analysts disapproved. When they attempted to restrict his teaching, he left the faculty at Menninger's and moved to Hartford, Connecticut, in 1953 where he treated and taught patients and students, myself included. Because of ostracism by the local orthodox psychoanalytic community, he moved to Los Angeles in 1959 where he died suddenly of a heart attack in 1961 at age 68.

Ruth Kaiser, his widow, sent me his unpublished book, and I was able to publish an anthology of his published and unpublished English works (Fierman 1965). Because a relatively small number of therapists in the United States have adopted his therapy in their practice, Kaiser's work remains unknown to most psychotherapists. The book presented here is a sequel to the earlier publication of Hellmuth Kaiser's work and also presents a distillation of my personal experience treating patients with psychotherapy. The book reviews the Kaiserian model of psychotherapy and then presents its application to a variety of settings, groupings, diagnoses, and circumstances, including managed care.

My career as a psychotherapist, which began in 1950 in my first year of Yale residency training in psychiatry, has included the psychotherapeutic treatment of hundreds of patients since then. Many teachers (particularly Hellmuth Kaiser), supervisors, consultants, and much reading were involved in my learning effective psychotherapy. In addition, I have taught effective psychotherapy to many students and clinicians. I am indebted to my teachers, patients, students, and colleagues, all of whom have contributed to the development of the concepts and perspectives about psychotherapy presented here.

The propositions about psychotherapy in this book

may or may not seem new or original to the reader. Most models of psychotherapy have both similarities and differences. The system of psychotherapy presented here is original only in the sense of being an idiosyncratic integration and presentation of what I have learned and experienced about psychotherapy. Sigmund Freud and Hellmuth Kaiser were my two main influences on basic perspectives and theory about behavior, pathology, and treatment. However, over the years, patients became the most important determinants of my practice of effective psychotherapy. Their positive responses reinforced and influenced my efforts, assumptions, and hypotheses, and helped modify and evolve the system of psychotherapy I now practice and teach and present here.

The subtitle *Effective Psychotherapy* is not meant to imply that other brands of psychotherapy are not effective or are less effective. Rather, it is meant to espouse the point of view that all psychotherapies should be evaluated from the standpoint of effectiveness and that the major concern of therapists should be the question of effectiveness. The term *psychotherapy* would best be used and defined generically as meaning any and all formal psychological treatments of psychological disorders in people. All clinicians practicing psychotherapy should characterize their therapy in behavioral terms rather than in terms of distinctive trade names, brands, schools, or charismatic teachers. The appropriate concern of clinicians should be to identify the conditions for maximum or optimum effectiveness of psychotherapy, namely, what kinds, categories, approaches, and strategies of psychotherapy will "cure" the most patients, most efficiently, quickly, and thoroughly.

However, in view of the chronically chaotic state of affairs in the field of psychotherapy, clinicians cannot escape the need to identify or label in one way or another whatever brand of psychotherapy they happen to be using. The therapy presented here can be identified or labeled in several ways, namely, Kaiserian, existential, humanistic, relationship, communicational, interpersonal, interactive, or even transactional. *Kaiserian psychotherapy* is probably the most conventional label to use because it clearly identifies the therapist and the therapy as representing and applying the teachings of Hellmuth Kaiser. A Kaiserian psychotherapist might possibly use an admixture of other models of therapy as well, but his basic model would be Kaiser's nondirective, here-and-now, communication-oriented approach to the patient.

The disadvantage of the Kaiserian label relates to the point already made, namely, that psychotherapies should not be identified in terms of charismatic leaders, but rather in terms of the strategies, techniques, or approaches intended to provide maximum clinical effectiveness. In fact, Kaiser himself insisted that he was not a "Kaiserian," but rather a psychotherapist searching for the conditions of effectiveness. In addition, Kaiser's experience as a psychotherapist was limited, with rare exceptions, to dyadic office psychotherapy with psychoneurotic patients. The psychotherapeutic approach presented here is proposed to be effective with couples, groups, and families as well as individuals and also for hospitalized patients with a wide range of diagnoses, including psychoses, character disorders, borderline states, and addictions.

Existential psychotherapy would also be an appropriate label because this therapy defines the therapist as assuming an *existential position* relative to the patient. An existential position is meant to convey to the patient that the therapist's overriding concern and intent is to communicate and share with him the therapist's here-and-now, subjective experience of the patient's communicative behavior and the psychotherapeutic relationship and situation. The explicit responses of an existential psychotherapist frequently focus on a priori assumptions implicit in the patient's behavior, body language, or verbal transactions, or on the phenomenological aspects of the patient's attitudinal position relative to the therapy, the therapist, his own self, other people, or the world at large.

The disadvantage of the label existential psychotherapy is the likelihood of confusing this therapy with other therapies also claiming to be existential, but differing markedly from the therapy being presented here. These other therapies are existential only in that they define the task of the therapist as engaging in analytic and insight-promoting activity focused on the existential modes of the patient, rather than defining the therapist's task as simply offering the patient an "existential" experience with a communicatively sharing person. This is the crucial difference between the model of psychotherapy presented here and all the other brands of therapy that claim to be insight oriented or psychoanalytically oriented and that espouse analytic activities or behavior as the task of the therapist and/or the patient. For those so-called insight therapies, and they are the most common and prevalent psychotherapies being prescribed for patients today, the therapy situation is a place for therapeutic "work," a place for figuring things out, a place for recall and reconstruction of historical and causal events, a place for identifying "problems" and solving them, a place for finding out how the mind works, a place where the therapist is a benevolent teacher, guide, advisor, coach, surrogate parent, and anything but a nondirective, nonauthoritarian, nonavuncular confidant with no interest other than to have a communicative intimacy with the patient.

The first rationale for rejecting the insight model of psychotherapy is that empirically it is not effective as a therapy for basic psychological change. Every experienced psychotherapist will confirm that clinical change and improvement in patients simply cannot be correlated with insight or recall and reconstruction of historical events. Even Freud was described by Jones (1955) as terminating a patient's analysis because the patient wanted only to be analyzed but did not want to change. Some patients improve with insight, and some patients improve without insight, and many patients do not improve despite extensive insight into the pathogenesis and secondary gain of their symptoms.

The second reason for rejecting the insight-seeking analytic model of psychotherapy is that it promotes a relationship with the therapist that fosters dependency of the patient on the therapist. The relationship in analytic therapy, no matter how benign, is basically authoritarian, pedagogic, nonmaturizing, and antitherapeutic.

The label *humanistic psychotherapy* would also be appropriate for the therapy described in this book. The concepts of humanistic psychology are completely compatible with the attitudes, existential position, and nondirective, egalitarian, sharing relationship offered to the patient by the therapist in the system of psychotherapy described here. The patient is constantly related to in a "humanistic" way, namely, as a responsible, motivated, potentially creative and autonomous person who can be relieved of his symptoms and freed from the constricting effects of past experiences if only the therapy and the therapeutic relationship with the therapist occur at the frequency of meetings and duration of therapy required for "cure."

The problem with the label humanistic psychotherapy is again that other therapies have also been identified as humanistic although differing in basic ways. Humanistic psychology developed as part of the social protest movement of the 1950s against the mechanistic, analytic, biologizing, dehumanizing implications of Freudian and Pavlovian psychologies. It was charged that the Freudian/Pavlovian ideologies promoted an erroneously limited view of human nature and did not properly appreciate the distinctly humanistic qualities of personhood in human nature and the potential in all humans for developing altruistic utopian ideals.

The writings of Maslow about human potential (1971), Rogers about self-actualization (1961), and Buber about the I–Thou relationship (1958) were all seminal in developing the philosophical and theoretical foundations of the humanistic psychology movement. This, in turn, led to the evolving of new models of psychotherapy that were explicitly nonanalytic, nonauthoritarian, and nondirective. These therapies, particularly Roger's *encountering therapy*, turned out to be very similar to the psychotherapy evolved independently by Kaiser and me. However, some psychotherapies identified as "humanistic" are also directive, analytic, explicitly insight promoting and problem solving, and may even include physical interventions and manipulations such as BioEnergetics (Lowen 1958), Rolfing (Rolf 1963), massage therapy, and so on.

In Rogerian psychotherapy there are subtle but basic differences from the therapy presented here, although it is also essentially an existential, humanistic, and nondirective therapy. Rogerian therapy often seems to have a preachy, sanctimonious, or inspirational-directive quality. This element would not be compatible with the principles espoused in the therapy model presented here, namely, that a nondirective, nonavuncular, nonauthoritarian relationship is essential for maximum effectiveness in psychotherapy.

Relationship psychotherapy might be an apt label for our model, but it is too general, nonspecific, and nondiscriminating. With all the aforementioned considerations in mind, I have exercised my prerogative as author and have labeled this therapy simply as *effective psychotherapy*. I will proceed to delineate the model itself, namely, the principles, rationale, process, and application of this psychotherapy that I and colleagues have found to be more effective and successful than any other brand we have tried or observed.

For psychotherapists to have available to them a model of psychotherapy that holds forth the promise of effectiveness for a wide range of psychological disorders is the good news. The bad news, at least for therapists in the United States, is that for the past few years the practice of medicine, including psychotherapy, has been undergoing drastic change. Third-party payers have increasingly imposed so-called managed care control over the practice of medicine. The rapidly growing managed care companies have colluded with government, corporations, employers, and organizations to reduce the costs of health care by monitoring and restricting the provision of health services for their employees and staffs. They decide who the clinical providers will be and what treatments will or will not be approved for payment.

Psychiatric therapies have received the harshest restrictions, and psychotherapy is either denied completely or is reduced to a small number of sessions. Resistance to these restrictions from organized psychiatry and psychology has been ineffective partly because mainstream psychiatry over the past several years has been turning away from a psychosocial frame of reference to an organic, biological one with accompanying emphasis on organic, medical, and biological treatment approaches rather than psychosocial ones. Under managed care, psychopharmacotherapy and brief, short-term problem-solving or crisis intervention therapies are approved for payment, but long-term, cure-directed therapies are not. Quick symptom relief and improved social function are approved as goals of therapy whereas therapies seeking basic personality or character change are no longer approved for payment. The concept of full mental health has been discarded, and patients are left vulnerable to relapse and recidivism.

American psychotherapists face a major problem at this time, namely, how to help their patients achieve mental health rather than simple relief of symptoms, and how to practice effective psychotherapy in an environment of restrictive managed care that is, in fact, really "managed costs," often providing third-party payers with maximum profit by providing patients with minimum treatment.

There are no simple solutions to make the problems of restrictive managed care disappear. However, it is possible for psychotherapists to maintain a frame of reference that will provide their patients with the most effective psychotherapy that can be done under such limiting circumstances and yet does not compromise the therapist's own integrity or commitment to the patient's treatment. A major goal of this book is to help psychotherapists empower their patients to cope with the reality of unavoidable constraints imposed on their psychotherapy by managed care and to motivate them to continue to seek psychotherapeutic experiences that will foster improved mental health (see Chapter 5).

The concepts presented in this book can be useful first as a basic generic model of therapy with the potential for promoting full mental health. They also can be modified and adapted to meet less ambitious goals such as crisis intervention, short-term focused problem-solving therapies, or long-term supportive therapies for patients who for one reason or another are not candidates for definitive curative psychotherapy.

Full mental health is defined as being free of psychopathological signs and symptoms, maintaining maximum social adjustment, and being free from neurotic, psychological, and emotional constraints on one's creativity and achievement of one's full human potential.

One final note: for convenience sake in the Introduction and in the text that follows I have used the masculine pronouns "he," "him," or "his" whenever referring to the therapist or the patient.

1

THE UNIVERSAL THERAPY: COMMUNICATIVE INTIMACY

Kaiser's views on psychotherapy (1965a,b,c) were formulated as a triad of "universals," the term *universal* in this context meaning that the phenomenon, principle, or concept applies to all persons—past, present, or future. The Universal Triad consists of (1) the Universal Psychopathology (the fusion fantasy), (2) the Universal Symptom (duplicity in communication), and (3) the Universal Therapy (communicative intimacy). The Universal Psychopathology is defined as the *fusion fantasy*, an inborn ubiquitous fantasy present to some degree in all persons, involving varieties of magical thinking and functioning to blunt, dull, or deny the reality of one's individuality and psychological separateness and autonomy. It is the psychopathology that supports the full range of clinical dependency (see Chapter 3).

The Universal Symptom is defined as the communicative behavior pathology or disorder by which all persons manifest their fusion fantasy, deny or distort the reality of their separateness, and attempt to create illusionary fusion relationships with others, including their therapists. In psychoanalytic parlance, the Universal Symptom would be labeled *transference behavior*. Kaiser called it *duplicity in communication* (see Chapter 2).

The Universal Therapy is defined as the relationship of *communicative intimacy* offered to the patient in psychotherapy by the therapist. It is postulated that the only necessary and sufficient condition for effectiveness in psychotherapy is that the sole and exclusive effort of the therapist should be to offer, promote, establish, and maintain a relationship of genuine communicative intimacy. Because no other conditions are required of the therapist, the therapy would then become uniquely nonmanipulative, nonauthoritarian, nondirective, and nondemanding of the patient. It follows then that the only conditions required for the psychotherapeutic process to occur would be the physical presence, mental capacity, and communicative availability of the patient plus the communicative presence, communicative interest, and communicative activity of the therapist.

Kaiser (1959) proposed that psychotherapy not be conceptualized or identified in terms of abstractions about the patient's illness, state of mind, or response to treatment, such as is implied in the terms *insight therapy*, *resistance analysis*, or *cognitive therapy*. Rather he urged that therapies be conceptualized and identified in terms of the therapist's orientation, intent, or activity such as would be implicit in the terms *supportive therapy*, *relationship therapy*, *interpretive therapy*, or *communicational therapy*.

He also insisted that the therapist assume full responsibility for the conduct and outcome of psychotherapy (1955).

He rejected the traditional and conventional point of view that the patient is responsible, or at least partially responsible, for therapy outcome, or that the patient must be an active, motivated collaborator for the therapy to occur. Kaiser declared that the sole and exclusive effort of the therapist to establish and maintain a genuine communicative relationship of intimacy with the patient was the only necessary and sufficient condition for effectiveness in psychotherapy. He termed this effort the *Universal Therapy*.

RULES

In this therapy there are no rules for the patient and no rules for the therapist (other than commonsense conditions having to do with compliance with social and professional standards of clinical practice, e.g., ethics, confidentiality, clinical records, security measures, etc.). The psychotherapist, after initial arrangements and contractual agreements are completed in regard to appointments, fees, hours, and so forth, simply meets with the patient and, in the first and all subsequent hours, engages the patient in a nondirective manner. There are no rules or tasks for the patient other than to appear for therapy at the designated time. There are no rules for the therapist other than not to withdraw psychologically from the patient.

I frequently begin hours with a simple "hello" and then usually offer tea or coffee. In a first hour I may begin with a statement summarizing all I have learned about the patient from data provided by the referring clinician, from previous clinical records about the patient, or from the patient's initial phone call requesting an appointment. This is to clear the air and let the patient know that I do not intend to keep information about him from him. I frequently close my statement with the phrase "and that's all I know about you." I then wait silently and expectantly for the patient to take the initiative to continue the dialogue in whatever way he pleases, including silence if that is his choice. I may break the silence, if it occurs, by sharing my perception of the patient's appearance, body language, or obvious emotional state, or my feelings and thoughts about the patient's silence. Otherwise, I might simply share with the patient how I am experiencing his behavior and communications and my reactions to the content and manner of his communications. That's it. No interpretations, analyses, inquiries, requests for more data, exhortations, or admonitions. The ambiance or atmosphere of the encounter is nonstructured, nonstrategic, and nontechnique-oriented. Instead it is open to spontaneous interactive communication. The only requirement for the patient in this therapy is that he be physically present and psychologically available for a relationship of communicative intimacy. By that I mean simply that the patient not be asleep or in a coma, intoxicated, drugged, or otherwise organically or neurophysiologically precluded from engaging in a communicative intimacy with the therapist.

The therapist assumes full responsibility for the conduct of the therapy and, by relating to the patient in a nondirective manner, he does not provide the patient with tasks, responsibilities, expectations, or questions to which the patient can then choose to answer, comply, submit or obey, or, contrarily, refuse, disobey, resist, or defy. Thus, the therapist does not provide directive behavior that would reinforce the patient's propensities for a fusion or dependent or pseudoindependent relationship. The patient cannot in reality comply with or defy the therapist because the therapist places no demands or directives on him. The patient's therapy becomes simply what happens to him when he is with the therapist. The patient remains fully responsible for his own behavior in and out of the therapy, but the therapist accepts and claims full responsibility for the conduct and outcome of each hour as well as the entire therapy.

PREREQUISITES

The therapy presented here defines the task and activity of the therapist simply and solely as offering a relationship of communicative intimacy to the patient. Of necessity, this relationship must be sustained for as long as it takes to effect a clinical remission or cure or until the patient or his managed care insurance company terminates the therapy, a period of time not uncommonly requiring several months or even years.

Since managed-care-controlled health insurance will only approve or reimburse short-term or so-called brief psychotherapy, access to definitive, curable, long-term psychotherapy is rapidly being denied throughout the country to all insured patients needing such therapy. This has become a national crisis as yet unsuccessfully challenged by the leaders and representatives of the professional medical and mental heath communities. The limited options available to psychotherapists and their patients in dealing with the restrictions of managed care are discussed in Chapter 5.

A personal prerequisite for a psychotherapist to be able to provide long-term, definitive, effective psychotherapy is that he must have a compelling interest in engaging in prolonged, sustained communicative intimacies with people. Clinicians who do not feel comfortable with, do not enjoy, or have difficulty promoting or participating in prolonged communicative intimacies with people will not be successful with this brand of therapy. They do better as psychotherapists who practice brief, directive, structured, or analytic psychotherapies. It is our position that these therapies reinforce basic dependency in patients and that the gains made would be at best symptom removal without basic transformation of the patient's underlying personality disorder or character neurosis. The patient would be left vulnerable to relapse and recidivism or to suffering in the future from some related psychological disorder.

As corollary to the prerequisite that the psychotherapist be interested in having communicative intimacies with people is the requirement that the therapist not have attributes that would interfere with that interest, such as rigidity of thought or slavish adherence to dogmas about psychotherapy, including the promoting of insight, problem solving, and pedagogical or other authoritarian behaviors.

Similarly, the therapist must not have neurotic traits that would interfere with sustaining a nonauthoritarian relationship with communicative intimacy as its sole purpose. Anxiety, ambivalence, and sadistic or authoritarian tendencies would interfere with or even preclude the therapist's pursuit of an exclusive interest in communicative intimacy with his patient.

However, it should be noted that even practitioners of directive and authoritarian psychotherapies claim their cures and successes. It is our contention that even in such successful directive therapies there also may be a considerable measure of nondirective communicative intimacy. That activity is the potent ingredient that would account for successful outcome despite the directive and authoritarian behavior of the therapist.

An additional personality prerequisite for an effective psychotherapist is that he be endowed by nature or heredity, training or conditioning, or by some combination of these factors, with sensitivity and responsiveness to the phenomenon of duplicity in communication, the universal symptom of people in psychotherapy (see Chapter 2). In this therapy it is essential that the therapist be sensitive and responsive to the patient's overt and covert efforts to establish fusion—a dependent relationship with the therapist and others. A therapist insensitive to the patient's fusion efforts would inevitably reinforce the patient's fusion propensities and this would preclude a full therapeutic outcome.

Other prerequisites for an effective psychotherapist include sufficient training and experience to assure familiarity with psychopathology and behavior pathology, and competence in the art of performing psychotherapy. It also is desirable but not essential that the psychotherapist be a graduate and licensed mental health professional, able to negotiate efficiently the necessary arrangements for psychotherapy with patients, families, regulatory and licensing government agencies, third-party payers, and other components of the government regulatory health industry and insurance complex.

Needless to say, the practice of psychotherapy is not the prerogative of any one particular professional health discipline. Effective psychotherapists may and do come from the ranks of the clergy, medicine, nursing, psychiatry, psychology, social work, and other professional disciplines.

TASK OF THE THERAPIST

The single, concentrated task of the therapist is to offer the patient a relationship of nondirective communicative intimacy. Such a relationship would require that the therapist be authentic, egalitarian, nonavuncular, nonpedagogic, spontaneous, and sharing. The therapist simply shares his inner state, his cognitive and affective responses to the presence of the patient, and his associations to the verbal and nonverbal behavior of the patient. He has no demands to make of the patient other than to be heard.

The only constraints on the therapist making a full disclosure of all his innermost thoughts and feelings are commonsense ones. He would not share responses that he has reason to think would have a harmful effect on the patient or the therapy. Timing would be a factor. The therapist beginning a therapy would of necessity be more restrained and accommodating and would avoid what might be perceived by the patient as provocative or critical comments. The goal of the first hour should be to set up and make possible the second hour. Only gradually should the therapist provide the full dose of his innermost reactions to the patient's behavior and stories. Premature sharing may lead to the patient's flight from therapy. Similarly, if the therapist's behavior deviates too much from the patient's expectations, the patient may flee. As the relationship develops and the patient's confidence and trust are established, the therapist can increase the risk of opening and disclosing himself more fully and can move more persistently toward his goal of promoting a relationship of ever-increasing communicative intimacy.

The relationship of communicative intimacy characteristic of this therapy differs in one basic way from the relationship of communicative intimacy that may occur between close friends, lovers, or confidants: the relationship offered by the therapist is unilaterally unconditional. That is, the therapist does not withdraw or retreat from the relationship if and when the patient becomes unfriendly, hostile, or even nasty. In contrast to close friends, lovers, or confidants, the relationship offered by the therapist is unconditional. It approaches the relationship existing ideally between parents and children in which the love, availability, and positive regard of the parent for the child persist even in the face of negative, hostile, or rejecting behavior by the child. The basic rule for the therapist is that under no condition will he withdraw psychologically from the patient. There are, of course, some commonsense limitations to the therapist's commitment (e.g., violent or destructive behavior, breach of financial contract, etc.).

The psychotherapeutic relationship of communicative intimacy disavows and excludes all therapist activities or behavior unrelated to the patient's needs and interests. Therapists should not seek or use patients for self-aggrandizement, power striving, fusion relationships, acting out of rescue fantasies, or sexual gratification. Any lapse should be the basis for the ethical therapist to seek consultation, supervision, and/or psychotherapy and to refer the patient elsewhere unless the countertransference behavior is quickly brought under control.

Therapists should be aware of the masochism, passivity, and dependency that may lead some patients to encourage, solicit, or reward such abuses and incompetencies in psychotherapists. The greatest safeguard against the therapist submitting to the temptation of exploiting his relationships with his patients is for him to have a full, gratifying, sustaining personal life outside of his work with patients.

RATIONALE

Why should a meeting with a psychotherapist once or twice or maybe three times a week for 50 minutes affect how a patient's mind works, what his values and priorities are in life, and how he relates to other people, or alleviate his psychological or emotional symptoms, improve his social adjustment, and enhance his creativity?

Analytic therapies relate their successes to insight. This is the belief that once the patient finds out why he is the way he is he will cease and desist from being that way if only he truly wants to change. A fringe benefit of this concept is that failures in therapy can always be blamed on either not finding enough "why's" or else having a patient who "doesn't really want to change" or doesn't want to change enough to change. This theory is fallacious. Any experienced therapist who has used analytic, exploratory, or recall and reconstruction techniques can attest to having had many patients who did not change despite extensive and exhaustive insights and despite high compliance with the therapy.

So-called supportive therapies usually concede that although symptoms may be relieved by the supportive relationship offered by the therapist, the patient remains highly vulnerable to relapse once the supportive relationship is withdrawn.

The therapy presented here is nondirective and consists simply of a relationship offering communicative intimacy. The therapist offers a spontaneous, nonjudgmental sharing of his responses, reactions, and associations to the patient. The rationale for change invokes learning theory principles. That is to say, in this therapeutic relationship there is no reinforcement of the patient's fusion behavior pathology and there is positive reinforcement of the patient's non-fusion, reality-oriented, contact-need-gratifying behavior. (See Chapters 2 and 3 for a discussion of fusion behavior pathology, contact-need, duplicity in communication, and existential anxiety.)

OUTCOME

The outcome or result of any particular psychotherapy is a function of five variables: (1) competence of the therapist; (2) rigidity or tenacity of the patient's symptoms and behavior pathology; (3) frequency of therapy hours; (4) length of therapy hours; and (5) duration of therapy.

Competence of the Therapist

The competence of the therapist is a function of training and experience plus natural aptitude. Towbin (1978) has published data demonstrating the phenomenon of innate personality characteristics that can be found in completely untrained lay people. These people report that throughout their lives they have been sought after because they seem able and willing to provide spontaneous confidant relationships to others. Such natural relationships may have psychotherapeutic benefits and may be indistinguishable from the relationship of communicative intimacy occurring in effective psychotherapy. A major difference, however, would be that in effective therapy the relationship offered by the therapist is unconditional. Of course, the competence of a particular therapist may not be constant or may not be maintained for all patients, all diagnoses, or all aspects of an individual patient's behavior pathology. Countertransference, in the psychoanalytic sense, or "blind spots" or unresolved personality conflicts in the therapist may be aroused by thematic issues in the patient and may prevent the therapist from performing at his usual level of competence.

Rigidity or Tenacity of the Patient's Symptoms and Behavior Pathology

In therapy some symptom complexes prove to be only superficially entrenched in the patient's psyche and behavior and are relatively easily dissipated, transformed, or removed by brief or even mediocre therapies. Other symptom complexes, particularly character disorders, seem more deeply entrenched and resist prolonged and competent therapy. Theoretically, time, patience, and perseverance will eventually overcome resistance and cure all functional psychological disorders, but practicalities, including managed care, may preclude such a protracted course. A full or partial clinical failure may result simply because of the massive resistance of the patient's pathology.

It is generally assumed that character neuroses or character disorders are more rigidly defended by the patient as compared to symptom neuroses and pose more formidable resistance to change in therapy. Similarly, chronic psychotic behavior also manifests strong rigidity and resistance to psychotherapeutic change. However, it is a clinical myth that character disorders or chronic psychoses are untreatable or incurable by psychotherapy (see Appendix 1: "Myths in the Practice of Psychotherapy"). Difficult, yes; impossible, no. They only require more prolonged, intensive, and sustained effort than other less rigidly defended pathologies. In every clinic, practice, or facility where character disorders or chronic psychoses are treated by competent, ambitious, cure-oriented psychotherapists, clinical cures have been reported, albeit they are few and far between. It remains a matter of arbitrary individual therapist judgment when to conclude that an individual patient is, for all practical purposes, incurable and untreatable.

Frequency of Therapy Hours

Freud allegedly met with his patients daily, seven days a week, but psychoanalytic practice since Freud has gradually reduced the frequency of therapy hours to five, then four, and now three times or less per week. There are, as yet, no convincing data to establish on the basis of research what would be the optimum frequency for effective psychotherapy. Nor is there an empirical consensus among practicing psychotherapists as to what would be an optimum frequency for all patients or for selected diagnostic categories. However, there does seem to be a loose unofficial consensus that "more is better than less," that two sessions per week are better than one, and so forth.

Common sense suggests that to transform lifelong-held character defenses and to free the patient from basic personality pathology will require a more intensive therapeutic relationship than is feasible in a once-a-week therapy. Too much occurs in the patient's life experiences between single weekly sessions to dilute, distract, and neutralize the impact and influence of the therapy. I usually tell my new patients that three sessions per week would be an ideal way to begin their psychotherapy, with a decrease or increase in frequency to be determined after a trial period of one or two months. If this is rejected by the patient, I urge that we meet at least twice a week at the outset. Unfortunately, many patients claim financial hardship or limited coverage by their managed care insurance, and we then have to settle for a once-a-week therapy.

Length of Therapy Hours

The units used to measure and define labor in Western society are traditionally the work hour, the 8-hour work day, and the 5-day work week. These units are too deeply entrenched in the consciousness of contemporary psychotherapists to permit extreme deviation from them. The hour as the basic unit defining a therapy session seems to go back to Sigmund Freud. In the United States the therapy hour became formalized as a 50-minute hour, permitting the therapist to have 10 minutes between patients to make notes, to tend to personal needs, and so forth. Many therapists then took advantage of this tradition and began scheduling patients every 50 minutes in order to increase their case load and incomes. Soon the 45-minute hour became more the rule than the exception. Currently, psychotherapy sessions vary among therapists and are even reimbursed by insurance at designated categories of

15-minute, 30-minute, or 45-minute psychotherapy sessions. However, from a clinical point of view, flexibility rather than rigidity would seem to be desirable. All experienced therapists have encountered exceptions when extended therapy sessions have proven compelling and helpful.

A distraught patient should not be dismissed by the therapist simply because "time is up!" Nor should a breakthrough in communication with a previously blocked patient be interrupted simply because it occurs at the end of a session. Psychotherapy conducted in the context of crisis intervention frequently requires extended or even marathon sessions. However, most therapists experience fatigue and a kind of burnout if they meet consistently or consecutively with their patients for sessions lasting longer than 50 to 60 minutes. On the other extreme, common sense precludes the expectation that brief psychotherapy sessions will result in significant cures. Thirty-minute and 15-minute sessions may provide emotional support and may even achieve some symptom relief, but significant personality or characterological change will not occur.

Duration of Therapy

Most patients come to therapy seeking relief of symptoms and resolution of life problems. They rarely seek or welcome efforts to change or "cure" their character or personality pathology. They may know and concede their anxieties, depressions, or phobias, but they usually do not know or admit their psychological dependency, fusion-behavior, negativism, duplicity, pseudo-independency, defensiveness, evasiveness, intellectualization, insensitivity, or other character traits and defenses that maintain the rigidity and tenacity of their character and personality and resist change. Indeed, none of us can easily imagine what it would feel like to be a different person from what we are other than in terms of symptoms or established behavior patterns, just as we cannot easily imagine what it would be like to be dead or to experience "nothingness."

Thus, most patients terminate therapy once symptomatic relief has been achieved or social and interpersonal problems have been resolved, but long before character or personality pathology has been changed. This accounts for the dismal record of relapse characteristic of patients receiving brief or "problem-solving" psychotherapy. The full "cure" of adult patients with character disorders, personality disorders, or other significant chronic psychological disorders may require 3 to 5 years of intensive psychotherapy at a frequency range of 2 to 4 hours per week. Unfortunately, such a treatment is unlikely to be sanctioned in today's managed care insurance climate. As in all medical therapeutics, the proper dosage is enough to effect a "cure," and the individual patient, who is never the hypothetical average patient, may require more or less therapy than the average.

CURE IN PSYCHOTHERAPY

Cure in psychotherapy can be conceptualized as a clinical triad: relief of symptoms, optimum social adjustment, and enhanced creativity. The relief of symptoms and improvement in social adjustment do not necessarily require a basic transformation of the patient's character. The release or enhancement of the patient's creativity usually does require such a transformation.

What is meant by *cure* in psychotherapy? Neither more nor less than the meaning of the word *cure* as it is used in general medical therapeutics: the patient has become free of signs and symptoms of illness even though he remains always partially or totally vulnerable to recurrence of the same, similar, or related illness. The use of the word or concept of "cure" usually relates to the statistical probability of recurrence. Thus, symptom-free addicts or cancer patients are usually regarded as "arrested" rather than "cured" until several years have elapsed, whereas symptom-free patients treated for fractures or bacterial infections are regarded as cured because of the low probability of relapse.

Every illness represents a complex resultant phenomenon, reflecting the interaction between the forces of external or internal stresses impinging on the patient's homeostasis versus the forces of the patient's resistance/vulnerability factors. Some illnesses reflect maximum external stress versus minimum internal resistance, for example: traumatic injuries, gunshot wounds, poisoning, and so forth. Other illnesses reflect relatively minimal stress versus maximum resistance/vulnerability factors, for example: allergies, genetic diatheses, diabetes, congenital disorders, and the like. Most illnesses fall somewhere in between these extremes. So-called mental illnesses reflect symptomatic and maladaptive reactions to varieties of psychological stress. These are conditioned by faulty social learning during and beyond childhood interacting with inherited and acquired vulnerabilities and susceptibilities at the biochemical and neurophysiological level of functioning, including aberrations of neurotransmitter biochemical mechanisms at the synaptic cleft.

"Cure" as used here means relieving, changing, or removing the signs and symptoms of mental illness, restoring or establishing norms of psychic functioning, reducing the probabilities of future recurrence and relapse, and, finally, promoting previously unrealized potentialities for optimum psychosocial and creative functioning. Effective psychotherapy can, and does, achieve "cures" with mental illness; there is no scientific basis for the persistent myth that mental disorders are incurable. Recurrence, relapse, or new mental disorders may occur with any individual patient, and future stresses may not be prevented or eliminated, but, hopefully, stress tolerance will be increased and recuperative powers enhanced.

The goal of effective psychotherapy is to achieve the clinical cure-triad of (1) relief of signs and symptoms, (2) optimum social adjustment, and (3) enhanced creativity. The relief of neurotic symptoms such as anxiety, depression, dissociation, obsessions, compulsions, phobias, and addictive states is the most easily achievable component of the clinical triad of cure. This is because neurotic symptoms are readily influenced by the status of the transference–countertransference relationship between therapist and patient. Neurotic symptoms are manifestations of underlying character neuroses and are by their nature labile, interchangeable, and negotiable. Patients frequently appear willing to give up their symptoms in exchange for what they experience as nurturance and dependency gratification from the therapist. Symptoms may be reduced or removed by a wide variety of therapist interventions including psychopharmacotherapy, either directive or nondirective psychotherapy, suggestion, hypnotherapy, behavior modification therapy, authoritarian relationships, and chance experiences. Unfortunately, relapse and recidivism usually characterize the outcome of therapies that do not address or affect the patient's basic personality and character pathology.

Social adjustment is the second major index of psychological health or disorder and, like neurotic symptoms, it is also reflective of the patient's underlying character pathology. It may be more difficult to achieve, however, than symptom removal via psychotherapy. Trouble with the law, delinquency, antisocial behavior, crime, and poor interpersonal relationships are all examples of social adjustment pathology. As with neurotic symptoms, social adjustment may be influenced by a wide variety of therapist interventions, including both directive and nondirective therapies. As with neurotic symptoms, patients may improve their social adjustment in exchange for perceived approval, indulgences, and dependency gratification from their therapists. In addition, as with neurotic symptoms, relapse and recidivism are likely to occur unless the therapy successfully addresses and affects basic personality and character structure and releases human potential for integrated autonomous functioning.

The third and most crucial component of the clinical triad of cure relates to the patient's basic character structure, namely, the enhancement of the patient's creativity and the achievement of his integrated autonomy. Effective psychotherapy frees the human spirit and results in a person who is creative, loving, independent and comfortably interdependent with others, spontaneous and more fully utilizing his innate talents and aptitudes, and willing to take risks in pursuing personal, gratifying, and socially relevant interests. When this quality of cure is achieved, relapse does not occur unless the patient's threshold for stress is subsequently overwhelmed by unusually intense and adverse pressures of life.

In summary, effective psychotherapy can be regarded as curative if it results in a patient free of neurotic signs and symptoms, maintaining optimum social adjustment, and manifesting enhanced autonomy and creativity for at least one year following termination of therapy.

CASE VIGNETTES

An old joke has it that when automobiles first became available for sale to the general public, an old farmer in a small rural town entered a car dealer's store and, familiar with horse-drawn carriages, he engaged the salesman: "Sir, just how does this thing run without horses?" The salesman opened the hood of one of the cars and went into great detail explaining the principles of the internal-combustion engine, the ignition, throttle, spark plugs, electric system, lubrication system, and so forth. When done he turned to the farmer and asked, "Any questions?"

"Only one," the farmer said. "Just how does this thing run without horses?"

On many occasions when I have lectured or discussed with colleagues my views on effective psychotherapy, someone will ask, "Yes, it sounds reasonable, but exactly what is it that you *do*!" The question is problematic for me because telling stories of dramatic or entertaining interchanges with patients does not reflect the slow, gradual, somewhat pedestrian pace of actual psychotherapy as I practice it and as it is presented in this book. In fact, what is truly distinctive about this therapy is that the therapist is not "doing" anything other than being an interested confidant, sometimes sharing with the patient his own reactions to the patient's verbal and/or nonverbal behavior. This nondirective receptive presence of the therapist does not lend itself readily to description in case vignettes. However, I have included in Appendix 4 Kaiser's

1962 playlet *Emergency* that he composed to illustrate the therapeutic encounter. In addition, the following three case vignettes of my own may give the reader some practical idea of what this therapy is about. To maintain confidentiality, I have altered the facts of the narrative to remove any identifying features of the patients involved.

Case A: The Man Who Couldn't Say No

Steve was in his thirties, about 5 feet 11 inches tall, neatly dressed in a suit and tie. He wore thick-lensed glasses and was soft-spoken and timid in manner with a hint of fearfulness whenever he looked me in the eye.

"Please come in," I said, directing him from the waiting room into my office. As usual I paused at the door, waiting to see where this new patient would go, whether he would simply seat himself or wait for my direction. He chose to stand in the center of the small cluttered office and waited. "Where shall I sit?" he asked after a few uncomfortable moments.

"Anywhere you like," I answered. He slowly went over to the couch and sat. "Is it all right with you if I smoke?" he asked.

"It's all right with me, but I doubt that it's all right for you."

He smiled. "I guess you're right. I should stop someday." His movements were smooth and graceful, somewhat effeminate, as he lit his cigarette. "Where shall I begin?" I was silent. He paused, "I'm new at this. What do you want to know?"

"Well," I answered, "it's not that I want to know nothing, but there's really nothing in particular I want to know. Whatever you may want to tell me is OK with me." And so began a therapy that lasted over a year. We met twice a week for hourly sessions. He told me he had come for therapy because of increasing depression that seemed to make no sense to him. That is, he claimed he had no reason to be depressed. He reported that he was happily married to a violinist who played in the local symphony. He enjoyed his three small children, a son and two daughters, and managed a thriving manufacturing company. Yet his mood had become increasingly depressed over the past several years until he finally decided to seek psychotherapy.

Steve was the third of his parents' three children. His father was an attorney and his mother a housewife. He had worked as an administrative assistant for his uncle who had founded the company. When his uncle retired, Steve became the executive officer. His sister had died of leukemia before Steve was born. His brother, ten years older, also died of chronic leukemia when Steve was 8 years of age. Steve had met his wife at one of her concerts and, after a year's courtship, they married. He approved of his wife's career as a musician, and they were in agreement on the rearing of their children.

Steve presented his history spontaneously with no prompting from me. After about three weeks of passive listening, I began his next hour with the statement, "Steve, I've been thinking about your therapy with me, and my sense is that you have structured the situation here as being a place where you can come and work on the riddle of your depression by recalling and reconstructing your life history."

Steve appeared startled by my remark. "Well, isn't that what I'm supposed to do here?"

"No."

"Well then, what am I supposed to be doing?" he said with obvious annoyance.

"Well," I replied, "while you are not supposed to be doing nothing here, there is nothing that you are supposed to be doing here. You are free to do whatever you want to do."

Steve stared at me with disbelief and then said, "I think it's important that I tell you about my life so that you might find some connection between my biography and my depression. Isn't that what's supposed to happen here?"

"No. But you seem to find it hard to believe me when I say you are free to do whatever you want here."

Steve shook his head and then, to my surprise, went back to methodically describing the chronological story of his life. For the next several sessions I once again listened passively, puzzled by the contrast between his obvious depression and the blandness of his detailed description of a happy and allegedly trauma-free past and current life.

The weeks slowly passed until I finally decided to communicate my growing sense that Steve was withholding and denying all negative, traumatic, hurtful episodes from his life history. It was simply too good to be true. "Look, Steve," I said, "I find it increasingly hard to believe that your life has been as free of pain, fears, frustrations, rejections, and misery as you make out. Also, my sense is that your persistent searching for the cause of your depression is your way of maintaining your denial that you already know what your depression is about. You remind me of the old story about the drunken man observed by a passerby one night to be crawling around a lamppost searching for something. 'Did you lose something?' the passerby asked. 'My wallet,' the man replied. The passerby joined in the search. 'Are you sure you lost it here?' he asked. 'Not here,' the drunk replied. 'I lost it in the alley but it's too dark to see anything in there!'"

Steve seemed not at all amused by my story and instead became strangely silent for the rest of the hour. But, to my surprise, in his next hour he launched tearfully into a bitter description of his past life replete with pain, frustration, and emotional deprivation. He reported that his mother had decided not to have a third child after her second, Steve's brother, was born. When the child was 8 years of age, the pediatrician informed the parents that the boy, like his sister, had leukemia and would not live more than a year or two. They then decided to have a third child and Steve was born. The family doted on the sickly older son, and he responded by living ten more years rather than only two. But during those ten years he dominated and tyrannized the family, including Steve.

After his brother's death at age 18, his mother kept his room as a museum to his memory and Steve was not permitted to use it. Steve always regarded himself as being a "spare" child, born explicitly by his mother to replace the anticipated loss of her favored son. Even more traumatic, however, was the fact that Steve's older brother frequently forced him to perform and submit to homosexual sex. To deny his brother's demands was unthinkable in the context of Steve's early family life. His brother warned him that he would kill him should he ever tell anyone about his homosexuality, and Steve never did until his therapy with me. I received Steve's emotional confession with intense feelings of shock and compassion. "My goodness!" I said, offering him my box of tissues for his tears, "what a terrible burden for you to bear alone and so young."

Steve dried his tears and continued. He reported that at summer camp, after his brother's death, an older camp counselor also solicited homosexual sex and that somehow he felt powerless to refuse or to report the counselor afterward. Steve claimed that was the beginning of a lifelong pattern of feeling compelled to submit to homosexual demands from older men. He firmly denied ever initiating, seeking, or even enjoying homosexual experiences but claimed he felt powerless to say no.

He also seemed unable to explain how or why gay men seemed to be able to identify him easily as a likely sex partner. He seemed unaware that his effeminate movements and mannerisms were cues that encouraged homosexuals to seek him out.

When he joined his uncle's business after graduating from college, his duties included visiting and inspecting several satellite factories that were part of the company. A pattern developed whereby some of the managers of these factories who happened to be homosexual spotted Steve as a possible fellow gay and, despite his being their superior, would invariably ask him: "Would you like to inspect the boiler room?" Steve would always answer yes despite his allegedly wanting to say no, and they would then withdraw into the private seclusion of the boiler room. Steve would then be asked for sex, and he would again feel compelled to agree.

This all happened in the past when gays were in the closet and exposure meant disgrace, possible loss of jobs or status or families and, in some states, even criminal charges. It was also in the days when homosexuality was classified by psychiatrists as a mental disorder to be treated with psychotherapy. Steve reported that his secret life as a passive homosexual had become increasingly burdensome, guilt-ridden, and shame promoting as he and his own family grew older. His self-esteem had plummeted, and he had become increasingly depressed.

However, these revelations in his therapy only seemed to make Steve's depression and despair worse. I shared with Steve my frustration and feelings of ineffectiveness as his depression persisted and deepened. I offered to prescribe antidepressant medication, but he rejected this suggestion out of concern about side effects. However, I was able to express my complete faith in Steve's autonomy and capacity to free himself from compulsive passive homosexuality. I repeatedly tried to assure him that he was in charge of his life and could make whatever choices he wished. But Steve clung to his position that, somehow, he simply could not say no to those who solicited sex from him.

"Look, Steve," I broke out one day, "*you* are not your mind or your feelings or your impulses or your compulsions. You are your behavior! You are what you do! Do you want to be gay? Do gay things! Do you want to be straight? Don't do gay things. Do you want to say yes? Say yes! Do you want to say no? Say no! You can do whatever you want to do and be whatever you want to be as far as choosing your own lifestyle and sexual identity are concerned!" Again there was a strange prolonged silence for the rest of that session.

Over the following weeks I could discern some subtle changes in Steve's behavior and comportment. He became increasingly more forthright in his communications. There was more eye contact. He was less graceful and less effeminate in his movements. He would discuss problems and issues in his work and home and sought less advice or direction. Indeed, during many hours I had little to say other than to express admiration over his newfound managerial assertiveness: "Wow! It seems like you've really taken charge of things in your life."

Then one day he appeared buoyant, cheerful, smiling, and garrulous. "Guess what!" he reported, "I inspected a factory this weekend. The manager asked if I wanted to look at the boiler room and I said yes. We went there and he asked if I would have sex with him . . . AND I SAID NO!"

That was the turning point. Steve repeatedly acted on his newfound power to say no to all unwelcome overtures. His depression lifted. His self-esteem rose. His work life and family life improved. He became increasingly active in community life and showed leadership in promoting various community and philanthropic activities. He finally terminated his therapy with no relapse reported during the years that followed.

Clinical depression is frequently the way an individual avoids the extreme risk and high anxiety of trying to change the unsatisfactory status quo of his life. Depression promotes resignation and procrastination. Effective psychotherapy opposes the function of depression. The therapist's persistent rejection of the patient's concept that he suffers from compulsive behavior driven by irresistible impulses may help motivate the patient to resist his own depression, to concede that he is choosing his own unwanted behavior, and finally to make the decisions he claims he wants to make but felt powerless to achieve.

Case B: To Be or Not to Be

Father Wessler slumped in the reclining lounge chair in my office, facing me, clearly despondent. His downcast mournful expression contrasted with his freshly scrubbed appearance: trim, neatly pressed black suit, bright white clerical collar, rimless glasses, close-cropped black hair, clean-shaven, younger looking than his 42 years of age. He was silent, occasionally looking up pleadingly. Then, shaking his head slowly from side to side, he would resume staring sadly at the floor.

"You look deeply troubled," I said after about three minutes of silence. "You might find it helpful to talk about it." All I knew of him in this first hour was from his phone call the previous week asking for an appointment. He had explained then that he was a principal at a local Catholic school and had been referred to me for psychotherapy by his own priest and confessor.

Dabbing his tears with tissues, he finally began his story. He had fallen in love with Sister Louise, one of the nuns who taught at his school. When confronted by him, she had confessed her own affection for him. After a few months of discrete and platonic meetings, he then proposed that they renounce their vows and get married. She had rejected his offer because of her own intense commitment to the Church, and they now both lived in agony and depression over their unrequited, celibate passion for each other.

He went on to report that owing to his sexual frustration he was resorting increasingly to masturbation, which he had confessed to his own priest with much shame and guilt. His priest assured him that masturbation was no longer regarded as a sin by the Church but, rather, now was viewed as a psychological and behavioral disorder. He advised him to seek psychiatric treatment.

"You want to be cured of masturbation?" I asked incredulously.

"Yes."

"But masturbation is not a mental disorder," I said.

"Not a mental illness!" he exclaimed. "Then what is it?"

"Well," I replied, "though many people still regard masturbation as sinful, most enlightened people now regard it as a normal way to relieve oneself of sexual tension or frustration."

There was a long pause and then he suddenly cried out, "Well, what about wanting to kill myself! Is that a normal way to relieve frustration too?" He began to sob loudly. I was surprised and moved by his outburst and waited patiently in silence for him to stop weeping. "Psychotherapy is supposed to help people with such problems," I said softly as he gradually regained his composure. We then made arrangements to meet weekly.

In his next hour he launched spontaneously into describing his life history. I listened passively while over the weeks that followed he revealed that he had entered the priesthood because of a vow taken as a teenager. His father had been a severe alcoholic and also was violently brutal to his wife and only child when drunk. Young Wessler had prayed to God to cure his father's alcoholism, vowing to enter the priesthood if only his prayer would be granted. Shortly afterward, his father unexpectedly gave up alcohol with the help of a psychiatrist and Alcoholics Anonymous. Wessler kept his promise, entered a seminary, and became a priest at age 24. He specialized in academic teaching and finally became a principal at age 35.

Throughout his narrative he remained downcast, usually staring at the floor and avoiding speaking directly to me or interacting with me personally. "Father Wessler," I finally said, "I can see that you are painfully depressed, but the way you tell me about your interesting life calls to mind a cartoon showing a shipwrecked sailor sitting on an island shore facing a palm tree and saying: 'You know, Jack, if I didn't have you here to talk to, I think I would go out of my mind!'"

He looked up, puzzled. "What do you mean?" he said.

"Well, it's like talking *at* someone rather than *to* someone."

"I still don't get it," he said as the hour ended. Despite my comment, his impersonal indirect behavior did not change in subsequent sessions. I was not surprised since I know that frequently patients will deny or ignore the validity of a therapist's observation or confrontation, only to concede its validity at some future time. I compare this phenomenon with the planting of a seed that only flourishes long after its planting.

More disturbing to me, however, was my observation that his depression continued unabated and even seemed to be getting worse. He felt his situation was hopeless and reported that he was frequently thinking of suicide. I became increasingly worried and frustrated by my inability to establish a communicative intimacy with him, to lessen his misery, or to resolve his dilemma. He wept frequently, complaining that, although suicide was the only way out, even that was forbidden by his religion.

"If only I could get myself killed," he moaned. "That would solve the problem." And then, to my dismay, he began reporting that he was seriously trying to arrange an "accidental" death. "Today I walked in front of a truck while coming here," he solemnly reported, "but the truck stopped too soon." Then he resumed his weeping.

What to do? I feared that he might, in fact, get himself killed. Should I hospitalize him? I had offered him antidepressant medication but he adamantly refused. Finally, in desperation and without reflection, I suddenly and impulsively blurted out, "You just want to ruin my reputation as a therapist by killing yourself!"

Father Wessler appeared stunned. His weeping stopped instantly and he stared at me in amazement. "What did you say?" he asked. Despite my inner bewilderment and chagrin over having uttered such a nonsensical and bizarre statement, I felt, somehow, that it would be a strategic mistake to retract it, and so I simply repeated it.

"Is that what you really care about?" he shouted, all semblance of depression gone. "Your reputation! I'm trying to kill myself and all you can think of is your damned reputation! What kind of a doctor are you!"

I felt strangely exhilarated by his outburst and decided to ignore his question and instead to confront his suicidal threats directly. "Listen, Father Wessler, if you decide to kill yourself, that's your choice. But I want you to know that while I may end up crying at your funeral, I'll be alive and you'll be dead and gone, and that's the way it will be!"

The hour ended and he stormed out without a word as I sat there pondering about what had happened. I clearly had lost my cool, behaved impulsively, said things I never thought I would say to a patient and, what was strangest of all, I did not even believe what I had said. I did not think he was trying to ruin my reputation. The whole thing was ridiculous.

I finally reasoned in retrospect that I must have behaved that way as a desperate effort to break through the wall of despair that my patient had erected between us, to somehow make emotional communicative contact with him, to interrupt and redirect his inexorable spiraling into the depths of a suicidal depression.

When the patient appeared at his next weekly appointment looking distraught, I began: "Father Wessler, I'm sorry about what I said last time. I know very well that you have no wish to ruin my reputation and that is not my concern at all. But I was so worried that you might actually attempt suicide that I felt I had to say something immediately that would distract you from your suicidal despair. That statement was the first thing that came to mind, so I said it even though I knew it was not true."

He lapsed into a prolonged silence and after several minutes passed I commented, "You keep staring at me as if you were looking at Egyptian hieroglyphics and trying to figure out their meaning."

He laughed (the first time since his therapy began) and responded, "No. It's just that I find you very strange. Not at all what I expected when I decided to go into treatment. I don't know why or how, but I have been feeling less hopeless since our last session."

"Does that mean you are feeling more hopeful?"

"Maybe."

Though less depressed and more direct and personal in his behavior with me, he nevertheless continued obsessing endlessly about his dilemma. Should he give up on Sister Louise or should he continue to try to persuade her to join him in giving up their clerical careers. Increasingly I felt there was something unconvincing about his alleged impasse. Finally I shared my suspicion: "You call to mind a story about President Truman. It was alleged that he once said to his staff, 'I wish I could find a one-armed economist!' When asked why, he explained, `All the economists I consult with tell me that on the one hand I must do something to lower inflation, but on the other hand I must do something that will lower unemployment!'"

"So how does that apply to me?" Wessler asked, annoyed.

"Somehow you seem careful to give both sides of your dilemma the same equal weight so as to avoid making a decision. You procrastinate and seem to be hoping that I or God or something will come along to tip the scales and spare you from the anxiety you would feel taking responsibility for your decision."

During the next several sessions Father Wessler began to review his options seriously. He finally decided that while he still wanted to pursue a Catholic academic career, he no longer was sure he wanted to be a priest if it prevented him from marrying his beloved Sister Louise. He requested couples therapy for himself and Sister Louise and I agreed. After a few more weeks of their meeting with me together, they finally decided to ask their bishop to grant them a year's leave of absence from their vows with the understanding that if they still wanted to marry after one year, the Church would allow them to resign from their positions as priest and nun.

The therapy ended at that point. One year later I received word from them that they had married and were now happily working together as lay teachers in an out-of-state Catholic school.

The potent ingredient of effective psychotherapy is communicative intimacy. My sudden outburst broke through the impasse in our relationship and opened the way to his relating to me and to himself in an authentic, decisive way that permitted him to free himself from suicidal depression and total resignation to the extreme constraints of his monastic life. This is not to say that emotional outbursts are a key to effective psychotherapy, but rather that authentic, honest communication from a therapist eventually fosters a similar authenticity in the patient.

Case C: Surprises

Mary came with her husband for her first appointment. She had explained on the phone that she was unable to leave her house alone because of panic attacks that had developed over the past year. Her family doctor had prescribed antianxiety medication that helped some, but she still was too fearful to risk going outside alone. Her husband sat in the waiting room while she entered my office.

She was 36, pretty, plump, dark haired, well dressed, with modest make-up. She walked briskly past the lounge chairs in my office to the couch where she plunked herself down and, without looking at me, stared at the ceiling and asked, "Is this what I'm supposed to do here?"

"Well," I replied, "you are free to lie on the couch if you wish, but it is not that you are supposed to do that."

"Well, what am I supposed to do and why do you have a couch here if you don't want your patients to lie on it?"

"Well, it's not that you are supposed to do nothing here, but there is nothing you are supposed to do here. You are free to do whatever you wish while you are here. As for the couch, I use it myself when I feel like resting or taking a nap."

After several minutes of silent pondering, she began narrating her history. She was an only child of Polish immigrants; she was married to a high school classmate; they had two children, a son 11 and a daughter 9; she helped her husband manage their grocery store; her father died when she was 13; her mother lived alone nearby. Her panic attacks began a year before and became progressively more frequent and more intense, particularly when she was alone. For the past month either her husband or her mother had to stay with her. She agreed to weekly psychotherapy but rejected my suggestion that she consider a schedule of gradually increasing counterphobic maneuvers or exercises to overcome her fears.

The following sessions were noteworthy in that she continued to lie on the couch, avoided eye contact with me, spoke freely about her past life, and revealed that she was a devout Catholic. Finally, I commented, "Mary, although you seem to be comfortable here and speak freely to me, you clearly always avoid looking at me, as if you were afraid of me."

"It's not you I'm afraid of, Doctor, it's me. I'm afraid if I look at you something terrible will happen. I know it sounds crazy, but that's the way it is! What's wrong with me, Doctor? Am I going crazy?" With that she began to cry and moan and swab at her tearing eyes with her small handkerchief.

"No, Mary," I said softly as I handed her my box of tissues, "you are not going crazy, and psychotherapy is supposed to help people with problems such as yours. It might help if you can say what the terrible thing is that might happen."

"No, Doctor," Mary said emphatically, "maybe next week."

Actually, it took several weeks before, with much trepidation, Mary finally agreed to reveal her secret fear. Still on the couch and not facing me she explained, "I'm afraid that if I look a man straight in the eyes he will be immediately seduced!" And again she began to weep.

I was dumbfounded and speechless. Was my patient a closet schizophrenic, a so-called *pseudoneurotic schizophrenic*, or a hysteric, prone to believe in angels, devils, and magical powers? I decided on the latter and said, "Look, Mary, you are a very religious person, and religion does encourage people to believe in things that cannot be proved or even disproved scientifically. I believe your fear that you will seduce men simply by looking into their eyes is such a belief, and I am willing to risk myself in order to help you overcome that fear. I urge you to take a chance and look me straight in the face. I'm sure nothing will happen."

Mary slowly sat up with head bowed and gradually raised her head until she was staring me full in the face. "You see," I said excitedly, "there's nothing to fear. Nothing terrible has happened." And in that moment of triumph I sat back in my recliner more forcefully than I usually do and, to my dismay, the chair fell over backward with me in it. As I painfully got back on my feet I could see Mary's wide-eyed, white-faced look of shock, her worst fear seemingly confirmed. But, fortunately, only for a moment as she then suddenly broke out with gales of laughter at my discomfort and embarrassment. It was as if she suddenly saw the situation in its true comical light, and her compelling fantasy about seducing men with a look was instantly dissipated.

From that session on Mary sat in the recliner opposite mine and faced me while engaged in dialogue. She shared several other fantasies with me that were involved in her agoraphobia and panic attacks. She confessed to being attracted to her husband's younger brother who had just divorced his wife and was living close by. She feared that going out of her home alone would result in her going to see him and inviting an affair. She feared that being alone might result in tempting predatory men to come to her and assault or rape her. She feared that being alone might result in her becoming promiscuous, and the scandal would cause the death of her elderly mother.

Paradoxically, as each new facet of her agoraphobia reached expression and increased her insight into the dynamics of her phobia, her refusal even to attempt any counterphobic behavior became only more entrenched. "Mary," I finally said, "it seems the more you understand the nature of your fears and panics, the less you are willing even to try to be more self-sufficient and change your dependency on your husband and mother. It's as if you want to prove to me that nothing we do here will make any difference in your need for them to be constantly with you." She made no response to my statement and continued to come to her sessions accompanied by her husband.

In her tenth month of therapy she announced that because her anxieties and fears had diminished considerably, she wished to end her treatment even though she still insisted that she needed the constant presence of her husband or mother. "I'm as close to you as your telephone," I assured her, "and you can return to continue your therapy with me whenever you wish." She drove off with her husband as I felt some disappointment in the limited results of my psychotherapy with her.

One week later I received a phone call from her. "Doctor, I wanted to tell you that yesterday I woke and felt completely cured. No fears—no anxiety—no panic—no nothing! I drove myself all over town and feel great. I don't need my husband or mother to baby-sit me anymore. I want to thank you. I'm sure this would not have happened if it were not for your treatment of me."

I thanked her for her call. I've heard from her occasionally over the years and apparently there has been no relapse.

Sooner or later in the course of a psychotherapy unexpected and surprising events and revelations occur that change everything in the therapy for better or for worse. Such occurrences may affect the relationship between therapist and patient, the direction of the therapy, and even the outcome. The therapy situation is a microcosm of life itself, full of surprises and unpredictable events. The therapist should be flexible and open to the opportunities presented by these unplanned developments.

2

THE UNIVERSAL SYMPTOM: DUPLICITY IN COMMUNICATION

Kaiser (1965a) had observed that there was a specific communicative behavior, universally characteristic in varying degree of all his patients in psychotherapy. He labeled this behavior as "the universal symptom: duplicity in communication." The term *duplicity* was not meant pejoratively but, rather, phenomenologically. He claimed that *all* patients in psychotherapy communicate either continuously or intermittently by behavior that is indirect rather than direct, implicit rather than explicit, manipulative rather than expressive, and concealing rather than revealing. The neurotic individual seems to communicate in such a way as to give himself the feeling that he is not responsible for his own words and actions. The task of the therapist is to behave in such a way as to promote in the patient a feeling of responsibility for his words and deeds.

Freud (1905) also had described this behavior when he wrote, "He that has eyes to see and ears to hear may convince himself that no mortal can keep a secret. If his lips are silent, he chatters with his finger-tips; betrayal oozes out of him at every pore" (p. 78).

In the presence of a patient engaged in duplicitous communicative behavior (verbal or through body language), the therapist experiences hearing a kind of static or double-talk and feels he is receiving double and contradictory messages from the patient. Because the therapist's psychological "set" is to receive his patient with the intent, if not the expectation, to engage in the open and accepting mode of communicative intimacy, the therapist reacts to the patient's duplicitous communication with mounting tension and discomfort. He experiences the patient's lack of genuineness and straightforwardness as distrust, rejection, and manipulation.

Kaiser also observed that when the therapist consistently and persistently responds to the patient's duplicity in communication with nonduplicitous sharing of his own inner subjective state and responses, sooner or later the patient's duplicitous behavior lessens and even disappears, to be replaced by genuine communicative intimacy between therapist and patient. Even more gratifying to the therapist is when a correlation occurs between the patient's shift from duplicitous to nonduplicitous behavior and the lessening of the patient's symptoms, improvement in the patient's social adjustment, and enhancement of the patient's autonomy and creativity, that is, the clinical triad of "cure."

Conversely, it appears that when the patient's duplicity in communication worsens there is usually a correlative worsening of the patient's symptoms, social adjustment, and dependency. These observations and inferences became the empirical basis for Kaiser's conceptualization of a Universal Therapy, that is, communicative intimacy. Kaiser postulated that the Universal Symptom, duplicity in communication, was but one behavioral manifestation of a Universal Psychopathology, the fusion fantasy (see Chapter 3).

More precisely, Kaiser proposed that duplicity in communication along with many other signs and symptoms of functional psychological disorder all serve to promote and maintain fusion relationships. Duplicity of communication in therapy is the patient's way of attempting to establish a fusion relationship with the therapist; to create an illusion of psychological fusion; to blunt, blur, or deny their separateness; to make the therapist appear to be the focus and source of the patient's decision making; and to make the therapist appear to be responsible for the patient's functioning and life experiences.

A patient once sternly warned me: "If I fail the test I have to take tomorrow because of my anxiety I will hold you personally responsible!" Indeed, he did fail the test and did quit his therapy!

With another patient, an unhappy wife, I had occasion to comment at the end of an hour that I had noted in the several weeks of her therapy so far that she had never stated why she remained married to such a nasty husband. She was silent as she left. On her next appointment she began the session stating proudly: "I did what you suggested last hour and told my husband to leave!" Apparently she had done this despite being totally dependent financially on her husband, who promptly abandoned her and their child and left the state.

Another patient always referred to his many relatives and acquaintances by their first names as if he had reason to assume I would know who they were. Long silences, wordless weeping, and other forms of nonverbal and body language are also examples of how the patient frequently attempts to create the illusion that the therapist can read his mind and is in a state of psychological fusion with him.

Duplicity in communication by patients in psychotherapy frequently is manifested by the patient's behaving in such a way as to try and make the therapist appear to be a surrogate parent who will advise, nurture, rescue if necessary, and be responsible for the patient's decisions and conduct. Freudian psychoanalysis terms this behavior as *transference*. Therapists, being human, are also tempted frequently to treat their patients as if they were their children, needing guidance, nurturance, and direct assistance with problem solving. Psychoanalysis terms this behavior as the analyst's *countertransference*. Therapists should be vigilant and firm in their rejection and avoidance of countertransference behavior, which is another variation of fusion behavior. To indulge in such behavior is to promote and reinforce the patient's basic dependency, no matter how helpful the therapist may be in problem-solving.

However, I am sure that if any of my former or current patients read this they will recall instances when I also offered advice or engaged in directive behavior. To this I can only say that the temptation to engage in fusion relationships is ubiquitous and that therapists, including myself, are not immune. Of course, in crisis situations therapists may be compelled to deviate from the ideal of nondirective behavior, but in such a case the patient should be informed that crisis interventions by the therapist are not the psychotherapy the patient needs for full psychological liberation.

In summary, the Universal Symptom of duplicity in communication is manifested by all patients in psychotherapy. The therapist experiences the patient's duplicitous communication with subjective discomfort as being behavior that is dishonest, manipulative, and lacking credibility. Patients in psychotherapy seem to prefer duplicitous over genuine communication; they do not seem to say what they really mean or mean what they are saying. Over time the individual patient's Universal Symptom seems to take on a consistent predictability and configuration, a character style or trademark, recognizable as part of the patient's general character pathology and reflecting the patient's distorted attitudes, values, and dependency. The patient resorts to duplicitous communication to avoid an egalitarian relationship and an open communicative intimacy with the therapist.

3

THE UNIVERSAL PSYCHOPATHOLOGY: THE FUSION FANTASY

Psychotherapists who treat patients by offering a relationship of nondirective, nonauthoritarian communicative intimacy do so out of conviction that this therapy is the best and most effective psychotherapy for psychological disorders. They usually arrive at this conviction on empirical grounds, either by being successfully treated themselves by such a therapy and/or by finding that they are more successful with their patients when they practice this therapy than they were using other models or "brands" of therapies. But professional clinicians are rarely satisfied with empirical therapies and seem to need a more scientific rationale for their therapies no matter how effective they may be empirically.

Kaiser (1955) offered in his monograph *The Problem of Responsibility in Psychotherapy* a loose framework of concepts that serve as a basis for his theory of psychopathology and behavior pathology, including the Universal Symptom: duplicity in communication (see Chapter 2). He proposed that "the fantasy of fusion" was to some degree a universal psychopathology, present in all humans. He defined *fusion* as the denial of separateness either by psychologically incorporating oneself into another person or by incorporating another person into oneself, thus either losing the sense of one's own autonomous personality or, by denial, destroying the sense of the other person's autonomous personality. The neurotic patient, or the neurotic aspect in all persons, seeks fusion relationships characterized by the Universal Symptom of duplicity in communication. Fusion relationships belie the separateness and autonomy of one and another's personality.

Kaiser's theory of the fusion fantasy being a ubiquitous element in everyone's psyche is consistent with psychoanalytic theory. Freudian theory (1923) proposes that at birth an infant is endowed with a primitive psychic apparatus with the propensity for subsequent maturation and development into differentiated and autonomous psychic structures identified by their functions as id, ego, and superego. Instinctual energies are represented in the psychic apparatus as motivational forces that have been identified as drives, namely, the sexual or libidinal drive and the aggressive drive. The ego is defined as the psychic organization for the service of adaptation with diverse mechanisms for maintaining intrapsychic harmony or homeostasis, while simultaneously developing behavioral patterns for obtaining instinctual gratifications from the environment and for coping with frustration and deprivation.

The ego, according to Freudian theory (Freud 1923), has at its disposal the mechanism of producing wish-fulfilling fantasies to help the individual cope and adapt to various degrees of stress, frustration, or deprivation. Thus, individuals, when experiencing deprivation or frustration of their needs or desires, may fantasize about those needs or desires, such as sex, food, freedom, success, power, or fame. Similarly, the infant or child may react to frustration or deprivation with fantasies that are autistic, delusional, or grandiose. These fantasies represent the wish of the child to maintain an infantile, dependent relationship with parental figures toward whom the child feels fused, controlled, and magically related. The fantasy of fusion makes it possible for the growing individual to cope with the ever-increasing demands placed upon him by his environment and the people in it during the prolonged period of shift from the infantile state of total dependency to the adult state of potential self-sufficiency.

Piaget (1952) has described the magical fantasies expressed and acted out by children in regard to their conception of themselves and the world and people around them. Freud (1914) characterized this infantile way of thinking as *primary process thinking* and this infantile orientation as *narcissism*. Piaget reported that magical thinking is prominent in the orientation of children until the age corresponding with latency and the prepubertal phase of psychosexual development. Then, apparently, the child's new experiences of increased socialization, sharing ideas with others, and having communicational relationships all lead to a major transition from magical thinking to more realistic and logical thinking and behavior in the growing child.

Of course, this only happens if circumstances are optimal in providing opportunities for the child to develop full and free genuine communicative intimacies and interactions with other healthy non-fused people. Then the child is more likely to grow up to become a mature, psychologically healthy adult. If such maturizing circumstances are not part of the child's experience, his infantile alogical thought processes persist uncorrected. Continued frustrations and deprivations will promote and reinforce his primitive fantasies of magical fusion with parental figures and their surrogates. The child will then maintain his distorted perception of his psychological separation from others. A basis is laid for subsequent development of neurotic symptoms, including the effort to create an illusion of psychological fusion with others by means of fusion behavior and duplicity of communication.

Thus, the two preconditions for psychoneurotic psychopathology and behavior pathology are (1) failure of maturation and development of reality-oriented thought processes and persistence of infantile magical thinking, including the fantasy of fusion with parental figures and surrogates; and (2) subsequent frustration and deprivation leading to increased neurotic symptom formation derived from other infantile wish-fulfilling fantasies. In short, the assumption may be made that symptom neuroses occur only in individuals whose thinking and orientation remain infantile with the persistence of magical fantasies of fusion with other people or other external or internal magical forces, that is, Satan, demonic possession, irresistible impulses, chemical imbalance, aberrant neurotransmitters, the unconscious, and so forth.

Neurotic symptom formation may be viewed as occurring when an individual's unique life-conditioning experiences fail to lessen or prevent the persistence of the fantasy of fusion. The individual would then be prone to react to stress, frustration, or deprivation with neurotic symptom formation. Symptoms may also occur in childhood as a consequence of the failure to develop adequate critical, perceptual, or judgmental faculties needed to perceive and accept the reality of separateness.

Additional opportunities for corrective socialization and improved communication may occur in adolescence; however, if the fusion fantasy and its accompanying fusion behavior and neurotic symptomatology have not been significantly dispelled by early adulthood, the individual's character formation will become progressively rigid and crystallized around the infantile orientation of fusion. The individual's fusion behavior may then become a lifelong state unless undone by successful formal psychotherapy or fortuitous psychotherapeutic encounters in real life.

Conversely, individuals having a mature, realistic orientation about themselves and their relationships with others are not driven by the fantasy of magical fusion or other alogical thought processes that can give rise to neurotic manifestations. Consequently, mature individuals tend to reject or to be repelled by neurotic individuals seeking fusion relationships. This reaction causes more frustration and separateness for the neurotic person.

In psychotherapy the fantasy of fusion is manifested behaviorally in patients by distortions of communication characterized by Kaiser as *duplicity in communication*. Correction, or lessening, of the communication disorder tends to heighten the critical faculties of the ego and to lessen or remove the fantasy of fusion. This process facilitates the development of mature adaptive behavior and the dissipation of accompanying neurotic symptoms or manifestations.

Because the illusion of fusion is reinforced by relationships in which the patient can feel either submissive or dominant, it follows that psychotherapy should be free of any authoritarian or indulgent behavior by the therapist and, instead, should provide maximum opportunity for authentic, genuine communication that concedes and does not blur the reality of the separateness of the patient and the therapist. Rules, directives, prohibitions, exhortations, advice, teaching, or preaching will all gratify and reinforce the patient's wish for fusion and dependency. Conversely, a sustained, responsive, spontaneous, egalitarian, realistic, accepting yet intrusively reflective approach by the therapist will gradually permit, foster, and reinforce the developing psychological maturation of the patient. This is the Universal Therapy proposed by Kaiser, that is, communicative intimacy offered by the therapist dissipates and overcomes the patient's Universal Symptom of duplicity in communication derived from the patient's Universal Psychopathology of the fusion fantasy.

In summary, the Universal Psychopathology is the fantasy of fusion, a fantasy shared by all humans, namely, that one is *not* really separate, independent, undirected, and in control and responsible for self. Instead, the fusion fantasy permits the individual to feel connected, dependent, and controlled by external or internal magical forces.

THE FUNCTION OF THE FUSION FANTASY

Kaiser proposed that the function of the fusion fantasy and resultant fusion behavior was to attempt to resolve a basic universal dilemma: how to achieve contact–need gratification without arousing awareness-of-separateness anxiety (existential dread). He postulated that all humans (as well as all other mammals) have a basic need for communicative contact with other members of their species in order to achieve optimum psychological maturation and development and to maintain optimum psychological functioning.

This conceptual construct of a basic human need for communicative contact with other humans is supported by various research findings. Studies of socially deprived infants (Spitz 1965), puppies isolated at birth (Hebb 1949), monkeys isolated at birth (Harlow and Mears 1979), the child–mother attachment (Bowlby 1969), the clinging reflex in newborns, and sensory deprivation studies all support the hypothesis of a basic contact-need in humans. In addition, children and adults in prolonged isolation frequently hallucinate delusional contact with imaginary others.

This basic need for contact may, indeed, be the initial source of the fusion fantasy, because all infants and children experience frequent separation anxiety and compensate for this with delusional fantasies of magical contact or fusion with their mother or other significant others. The infant requires direct physical and sensory contact with other people for normal psychological development. The growing child also requires direct, communicative, verbal, physical, sensory, and social contact with other people for normal psychological maturation and development. Even adults require communicative contact with others for normal psychological functioning. Contact–need deprivation at any age seems to have the potential to promote the illusion of fusion as the individual fantasizes or even hallucinates contact with others.

In adults, the psychic capacity for symbolic representation of actual object relations allows for some degree of contact–need gratification by means of hallucinatory or fantasied contact or fusion not only with other persons but also with symbolic or ideational psychic representations of other persons, such as abstract concepts, ideologies, or magical forces. The fantasy of fusion and denial of autonomy can be inferred as operative in persistent adult behaviors that Kaiser (1965b) has classified as:

1. *Childlike*: People who avoid presenting themselves seriously, minimize important matters, deprecate themselves, and deny their adulthood through silliness or buffoonery.
2. *Passion-dominated*: People who deny self-control, participate in mob actions, claim irresistible impulsive behavior, or join noble causes or patriotic movements.
3. *Fate-dominated*: People who invoke karma, fate, or destiny to account for their behavior through either fanatic beliefs or passive resignation.
4. *Reason-dominated*: Intellectualizing and obsessional people who deny personal choice or personal responsibility by invoking logic and reason as the determining forces of their behavior.
5. *Moral-dominated*: Religious fanatics, pseudopatriots, hyperscrupulous people who invoke duty or taboo to account for their personal choices and behavior.

Kaiser postulated that a major obstacle in the way of obtaining contact–need gratification was the anxiety engendered by the subjective awareness of each individual that in order to achieve genuine contact with an "other," one had to concede the reality of separateness from the "other." He maintained that only genuine communicative behavior could bridge the existential separateness between people. However, all people seem to experience some anxiety (existential dread) when they experience their own separateness, autonomy, and individuality.

Thus, the price all people must pay for seeking realistic contact–need gratification from others is to heighten their awareness of separateness and to experience some degree of *existential dread*. Existential dread is the anxiety that all humans feel to some degree whenever they experience their aloneness and independence. The philosopher Kierkegaard (1844) posited that all individuals always experience some anxiety whenever reminded of the eternal human verities and existential mysteries. What are we doing here? What is creation? Why are we here? What is the meaning or purpose of life? What is death? What happens after death? Where did we come from? How can something be created from nothing? These and other existential questions all arouse some degree of anxiety in humans.

The fusion fantasy is a form of magical thinking that relieves some of the anxiety provoked by these existential questions by presenting magical, spiritual, religious, mystical, and supernatural answers to them. The fusion fantasy permits the individual to maintain the comforting notion that we are all here as part of a grand universal scheme or cosmic plan activated by a divine intelligence that designs and controls all events of creation including our life experiences. We are not alone or truly separate beings! We are all connected or fused to supernatural forces. No one really dies! There is life after death through heavenly existence or reincarnation, and so forth.

Humans are compelled to seek contact–need gratification from other humans. Genuine communicative contact with others concedes and accepts the separateness that can only be bridged by communication. But awareness of the reality of separateness produces anxiety. For many people that anxiety is extremely painful and frightening, and they will avoid it by attempting to establish fusion relationships. Fusion relationships create the illusion of magical bonds, magical control, and denial—or at least a blunting of the awareness of separateness and its accompanying anxiety.

In summary, a non-neurotic individual with normal stress tolerance will seek contact–need gratification with others with a minimum of denial or distortion of the reality of separateness. He will avoid and reject fusion relationships, engage in nonduplicitous communication, tolerate the existential anxiety that accompanies his awareness of separateness, and seek nonfusion relationships to avoid loneliness (not to be confused with the anxiety of existential separateness) and to gratify his basic need for contact with others.

In contrast, the individual burdened with neurotic psychological disorders, including low stress tolerance, will desperately seek contact–need gratification also, but will avoid genuine, authentic nonfusion relationships. Instead, he will seek fusion relationships that will lessen or dull his awareness of separateness, avoid or lessen existential anxiety, but increase the pain of actual aloneness and frustrate the need for genuine contact (Kaiser 1965c).

In formal effective psychotherapy or in natural or spontaneous therapeutic life experiences, the fusion-prone individual may, over time, gain increased tolerance and acceptance of existential anxiety, give up his efforts to establish fusion relationships, achieve genuine contact with others, give up duplicitous communication, and experience the cure triad of (l) alleviation of neurotic symptoms, (2) improvement of social adjustment, and (3) increased achievement of his potential for creative, autonomous, independent living.

4

APPLICATION/ GUIDELINES

The model of psychotherapy presented here was originally designed for open-ended, "cure"-directed, outpatient treatment of individual, nonpsychotic, motivated adult patients. However, it can also be regarded as a generic brand of therapy that can be adapted and modified to provide focused, short-term, or limited goal treatment or crisis intervention. It can also be modified to treat couples, families and groups, hospitalized patients, psychotic patients, resistant or nonmotivated patients, as well as children, adolescents, and geriatric patients. In addition, it can be adapted for supervision, consultation, and teaching of psychotherapy.

The basic issue involved in modifying this psychotherapy for the treatment of variations in clinical diagnoses, groupings, and circumstances has to do with the degree of directiveness versus nondirectiveness required by the therapist. Ideally, psychotherapy would be as free as practicable of any directive activity by the therapist in order to avoid supporting and reinforcing dependency and fusion behavior. However, the reality of treating patients under less than ideal conditions requires some degree of directiveness, control, structure, and strategic intervention.

LONG-TERM VS SHORT-TERM THERAPY

Psychotherapy in which the therapist offers a nondirective relationship of communicative intimacy as definitive, "cure"-directed treatment is by its nature long term, usually lasting many months or even years. However, this does not necessarily mean that this therapy is prescribed to be long term; rather, it is usually prescribed as being open ended. This means that the therapist is committed to continuing the therapy as long as the patient is willing and as long as the therapy continues to show promise for overcoming all the signs and symptoms of psychological disorder or illness and preventing relapse.

Frequently, however, psychotherapy that is offered to the patient as being "cure"-directed is instead terminated by the patient after only a few weeks or months of therapy, not because of total cure, maturation, or psychological and behavioral transformation, but because the patient has experienced symptomatic relief, early remission of illness, or even, possibly, a "flight into health." If the patient elects not to continue treatment, his wish and choice should be respected and accepted. The therapist should not discourage termination (other than for commonsense exceptions such as addictions, suicidal depression, or dangerous so-called impulse disorders). An encouragement or invitation to return to therapy anytime in the future is sufficient. Short-term or so-called *brief psychotherapy* in this context occurs as a spontaneous outcome rather than as a strategy of prescribed brief treatment.

The following clinical examples are presented not to illustrate psychotherapeutic interaction with these patients, but rather to illustrate spontaneous early termination of therapy by the patient once a major or presenting life problem was relieved. In each case I did not discourage termination despite the patient's being far from well psychologically. I only reminded them that they still had treatable psychological problems and that I would be available to renew therapy if they chose to return. My cliché farewell remark is usually, "Please remember, I'm as close to you as the telephone." Of course, some patients who quit prematurely do return after they experience recurrence of symptoms later.

Clinical Examples of Early Termination of Therapy by the Patient

1. A 32-year-old bachelor manager of his father's laundry, introverted, shy with obsessive fears of homosexuality, entered weekly psychotherapy. After 2 months he had the first date of his adult life, fell in love, became engaged by the fifth month of therapy, married in the seventh month, and was symptom-free and elected to terminate after 10 months. There was no recurrence known to me.

2. A 35-year-old housewife entered therapy depressed, irritable, insomniac, and hypochondriacal. Her husband

was a compulsive gambler. After one month of weekly therapy she reported that her husband promised to reform if only she would end therapy. The patient reported symptom remission and elected to terminate after her second month. There was no recurrence known to me.

3. A 28-year-old bachelor salesman with severe social anxiety entered therapy. He showed some improvement after one month's weekly therapy. The patient enrolled in a Dale Carnegie public speaking course, reported that his anxiety was relieved, and elected to terminate therapy after the second month.

4. A 40-year-old heterosexual, single male factory worker entered weekly therapy because of panic over recent homosexual fantasies. He completed three sessions of psychotherapy. A sudden remission occurred following my conveying that I did not regard his homosexual fantasies as proof of homosexuality. The patient, greatly relieved, elected termination. There was no recurrence known to me.

Spontaneous short-term psychotherapies such as these are commonplace occurrences. They are very different from the brief psychotherapy often prescribed in recent years out of a necessity to curtail costs or, even worse, because many therapists, for one reason or another, have abandoned or rejected the concept that patients can be psychologically cured and successfully freed from their lifelong psychopathology and behavior pathology. Such cynical therapists reject long-term therapies, particularly psychoanalysis, as being ineffective or impracticable or both. The brief psychotherapy they prescribe is actually an authoritarian, directive, counseling, pedagogic, avuncular relationship promoting symptom relief with medication, problem solving, and improved social adjustment without regard for basic personality change or character transformation, which they believe is impossible to achieve anyway.

The problem is that the brief psychotherapy movement, while welcomed by the insurance industry, the government, the pharmaceutical industry, and by many, if not most, patients and their families, nonetheless excludes the patient from experiencing more ambitious curative therapy and leaves him vulnerable to relapse. Their mutual goal of cost containment may be achieved, but only at the price of incomplete and less effective treatment.

A major contributing factor to the widespread abandonment of long-term psychotherapies is the extensive takeover of the health delivery system throughout the country by so-called managed care companies. These companies have contracted with government agencies, insurance companies, and health maintenance organizations (HMOs) to control, regulate, and monitor both inpatient and outpatient psychiatric treatment in order to control costs. (For a more complete review of the devastating restrictions imposed on long-term psychotherapy and how therapists and patients can cope with them, see Chapter 5.)

This is not to deny, however, that there are circumstances where short-term therapy may be legitimately and ethically prescribed, for example, when open-ended, long-term, or nondirective therapy is simply not feasible or practicable. Such circumstances may include limitations of finances, impending departure of the patient or therapist, or clinical crises involving patients with suicidal, homicidal, violent, criminal, or antisocial behavior. In such cases it may well be necessary or advisable for the therapist to withhold nondirective psychotherapy entirely, and instead to offer a directive, strategic, problem-solving, crisis-intervention relationship.

However, once again, the therapist should be aware that no matter how effective or compelling the decision might be to avoid long-term therapy, the patient remains vulnerable to future relapse. Directive short-term treatment is superficial by its nature and will do little to maturize the patient or free him from his basic dependency. It may help him to feel better, to solve some problems, or to deal with a current crisis. It will not change major character structure or lifelong behavior patterns. These were not formed in a brief period in the patient's life and will not be changed in a brief period of psychotherapy.

Unfortunately, the majority of patients in psychotherapy today are being treated with prescribed brief psychotherapy and are being denied access to open-ended therapy because of nonclinical reasons such as financial limitations; prohibitions imposed by managed care companies, insurance companies, and clinical institutions; and lack of skill and training of many psychotherapists. It is a sad fact that few psychotherapists today are being trained to provide long-term psychotherapy. This is, in part, a result of the current overwhelming emphasis on biological, genetic, and neurochemical perspectives of psychopathology and behavior pathology plus the ubiquitous use of psychotropic medications in treatment that characterizes the training of psychiatrists and psychologists today. It is also the result of negative attitudes among many mental health clinicians who disclaim the efficacy of long-term psychotherapy and who reject the validity of psychosocial perspectives that hold that mental illnesses are produced, at least in part, by pathogenic conditioning, traumatic life experiences, faulty parenting, and psychosocial frustration, stress, and deprivation.

Brief psychotherapy is also frequently prescribed instead of long-term therapy for some patients by clinicians well trained in long-term psychotherapy, psychoanalysis, or other insight-oriented therapies. These clinicians rationalize on fallacious and mythical grounds that these patients lack the criteria for benefiting from long-term therapy, and invoke such criteria as age, intelligence, education, motivation, psychological mindedness, and social class. However, these criteria are mythical and unfounded (see Appendix 1: "Myths in the Practice of Psychotherapy"). Patients should not be denied access to long-term psychotherapy because of them.

The future appears bleak for open-ended and cure-directed psychotherapy to be as it once was, namely, the core identity of a psychiatrist and a clinical psychologist. Now expertise in psychopharmacology has become the hallmark of a psychiatrist. Severe financial pressures and shortages in our expanding society have created the climate for seizing on new discoveries in brain physiology, neurochemistry, and psychopharmacology to minimize, ignore, and discount previous knowledge about learning, child rearing, conditioning, behavior development and pathogenesis, and the possibilities of psychological growth and transformation through psychotherapeutic relationships.

Dr. Gerald Caplan (Caplan and Caplan 1969), famed Harvard proponent of so-called social or community psychiatry, postulated that every 20 to 30 years a cultural pendulum swings between the psychosocial perspective about mental illness and the medical/biological perspective. The medical/biological shift is usually related to some new scientific discovery about brain or nervous system function or malfunction that is then generalized inappropriately to account for the full spectrum of mental illness or health. The discovery of the spirochete cause of syphilitic paresis led to the false assumption that all psychoses must have some infectious etiology. The discovery that niacin deficiency caused pellagra psychosis led to the false assumption that all psychoses must result from vitamin deficiencies. The current discoveries about the functions of neurotransmitters in the nervous system and the findings of new brain imaging techniques and the beneficial effects of psychotropic medications have all lent credibility to the emerging dominance of the medical, biological, and genetic perspective in current psychiatric practice. Caplan observed that within 20 or 30 years following such shifts, disillusionment with the extreme organic emphasis gradually occurs, and psychosocial factors are rediscovered. The pendulum of psychiatric practice then swings back to a psychosocial perspective.

Of course, the medicalizing and biologizing of psychiatric practice have considerable economic benefits. Medical psychiatry is less time consuming and less costly. Psychopharmacotherapy for psychologically disordered men, women, and children is quicker and cheaper than any ambitious psychosocial treatment plan. The saving in time, energy, manpower, and money is demonstrable and tempting to clinicians, government, insurance companies, and patients and their families. The temptation is to exaggerate the efficacy of organic treatments and to deny the value of psychosocial, reconditioning, cure-directed approaches. The economics weigh heavily against the survival of the practice of effective psychotherapy, which requires long hours of interaction between patients and highly trained devoted psychotherapists.

The same factor of economics favors the emergence of brief psychotherapy as the clinical psychotherapy of choice. Less time means less cost. The predetermined termination date set by managed care for brief psychotherapy imposes a directive, controlling, authoritarian cast to the therapy and precludes it from freeing the patient from his basic dependency even if extensions of the therapy are granted by managed care. The patient is free only to accept or reject the limitations of his brief therapy.

COUPLES AND MARITAL PSYCHOTHERAPY

The psychotherapy of couples is subject to the same decision considerations as individual dyadic psychotherapy. Should it be directive or nondirective, open-ended or brief, once a week or more or less frequently? In addition, should the therapist's primary allegiance and commitment be to both parties equally or to one or the other of the two patients? Should the therapist always see the couple together or at times see the patients individually as well?

Ideally the psychotherapy would offer maximum opportunity for both members to achieve freedom from psychopathology and fusion-behavior pathology with resultant relief of symptoms, improved social adjustment, and enhanced creativity as well as resolution of the conflicts in their relationship with one another. The primary goal of the therapy should not be to preserve the couple's relationship or save the marriage, but to free and "cure" both members of their psychological disorders. This ideal rarely is carried out. Most therapies of couples as practiced today are focused on the relationship and/or the marriage, and most therapies are directive and manipulative. Psychological exercises and formulas are frequently prescribed with the intent of improving the relationship, enhancing communication between the members, and promoting strategies for establishing and preserving domestic peace and harmony. On occasion, so-called sex therapy may also be included in the treatment plan for couples.

If, however, the therapist does practice effective nondirective cure-oriented psychotherapy with individual patients, there is no reason he cannot do the same with couples. The issue of agentry is relevant here; that is, the therapist must be neutral and evenly committed to both members in offering a relationship of communicative intimacy rather than being the agent of either one vis-à-vis the other. Identifying one of the members as the "identified patient" and the other as the "patient's spouse" or "significant other" is not consistent with this model of therapy. The therapist should offer, in effect, a psychological "ménage à trois" and ally himself equally as an intimate confidant with both parties. The therapy is open-ended and nondirective. The therapist shares his inner state and reactions to the couple. The goal is to free both members from their dependency and fusion-behavior pathology. If this is accomplished and the couple find their mutual interests are best served by continuing their relationship or marriage, so be it. If not, they may decide to end their relationship and go their separate ways, hopefully with friendship and mutual respect and fulfillment of whatever responsibilities they might owe each other.

GROUP AND FAMILY PSYCHOTHERAPY

Here again the various models and formal brands of group and family therapies can be categorized as to the degree of directiveness versus nondirectiveness. Most forms of group and family therapies as practiced today are directive, structured, and manipulative. The goals are usually to provide support, to promote communication, to solve explicit life problems, and to enhance awareness and insight into pathogenesis and behavior pathology, but rarely to provide cure, transformation, or freedom from neurosis for the individual members of the group or family. The traditional group or family therapist is usually authoritarian and directive, particularly in doing family therapy.

However, once again, if the therapist espouses nondirective curative psychotherapy with individual patients he can do the same with group or family therapy with some modification of the basic model of therapy. The nondirective group or family psychotherapist offers to join the group or family as an active member, offering a relationship of communicative intimacy to all the other members and inviting all the members to function as cotherapists with one another.

Whereas with individual therapy the therapist can and should control the pace and intensity of the sessions so as not to exceed the patient's tolerance for emotional stress, in group and family therapy the therapist is no longer in complete control of the pace and intensity of interactions between the members. The therapist must be prepared to intervene, if necessary, in order to protect those members of the group or family who are vulnerable to being traumatized by overly aggressive or hostile behavior from other members of the group or family. Thus, the nondirective group or family therapist must on occasion behave in a more authoritarian and directive manner than he would during individual psychotherapy.

Another modification necessary in doing nondirective family psychotherapy has to do with generational differences between the therapist and small children in the family. The reality of age differences precludes the therapist from offering a completely egalitarian relationship with small children as he would to the adult members of the family. It is my practice, however, to give priority to promoting an alliance with the children in the family undergoing family psychotherapy even before I engage the adult members. I frequently begin a first session with a family by asking the youngest member of the family: "Well, what do you think is going on with your family?" I then proceed progressively to the next older siblings present and save until last my interaction with the parents. However, as time goes on and a communicative alliance is established with both the children and the parents, I then revert to a nondirective stance in subsequent sessions and simply offer a relationship of communicative intimacy to all the members of the family without attempting to structure the flow of the sessions (see Appendix 3: "Family Therapy in Psychiatric Hospital Treatment").

INPATIENT PSYCHOTHERAPY

Theoretically, the application of the basic model of effective psychotherapy to the psychotherapy of hospitalized patients need not be any different from the therapy of outpatients or office practice as long as the psychotherapist has no administrative responsibilities or controlling functions over the patient in the hospital and is able to maintain unconditional confidentiality in regard to the therapy. Unfortunately, in current psychiatric hospital practice, cost containment and third-party and managed care controls have exerted major effects. Hospital stays have been drastically reduced, and great emphasis is placed on organic and psychopharmacological treatment in order to facilitate early discharge. While theoretically a therapist could still attempt to do effective psychotherapy in the hospital, current hospital practice would make this difficult.

Moreover, if the psychotherapist is required to become part of the clinical team responsible for his patient's care while in the hospital, the therapist's relationship with the patient becomes compromised. He is now perceived by his patient as being in the role of a parent surrogate, and the nondirective aspect of the relationship and the therapy is lost. The patient's basic psychopathology of dependency is now supported and reinforced by the reality of the patient's actual dependency on the therapist as a member of the hospital staff that makes all the decisions regarding the patient's hospital management and privileges, that is, medications, freedom of movement, passes, curfew, diet, visitors, discharge, and so forth. The patient becomes aware that the therapist is required to report information about his therapy to other members of the hospital staff, and that information about his therapy becomes part of the hospital record and a factor in staff decisions about the patient and his treatment.

There is no easy or complete way to avoid this complication. Even if the therapist is a so-called "attending clinician" to the hospital and not part of the full-time hospital staff, he is usually still required to document something about his treatment and to participate directly or indirectly in staff decisions about the patient. The issue of compliance or defiance with hospital rules and regulations is ubiquitous for all patients in psychiatric hospitals. It becomes of special concern with patients who are hospitalized involuntarily, either through pressure from family or employers or through a court commitment, and are resistant and uncooperative with treatment. Unless the psychotherapist can convincingly disclaim any participation in the involuntary hospitalization of the patient, there is little chance of being accepted and trusted as a therapist by the patient. Similarly, patients with behavior pathology such as psychopathy or antisocial personality, paranoia, or negativism or those who are otherwise engaged in power struggles with authority figures will not trust or accept a staff psychotherapist as being truly allied with them. The staff psychotherapist is always identified by such patients as being part of the authoritarian system with which they are in lifelong opposition no matter how much the therapist disclaims it.

Theoretically, the problem can be minimized, if not eliminated altogether, by arranging for the psychotherapist to be excused by the hospital from all involvement with administrative responsibilities or decisions regarding his patient. However, the concept of the clinical team reporting and sharing in all decisions affecting the patient's treatment plan has become so ingrained in psychiatric hospital practice that it is highly unlikely that any current staff would ever agree to a therapist/administrator split that would require the patient to have two clinicians assigned to his care: one, an administrative therapist, responsible for all decisions concerned with the patient's management while in the hospital; the other, the patient's psychotherapist, responsible only for the patient's psychotherapy and permitted unconditional confidentiality of the therapy. For further discussion of inpatient group and family therapy see Appendix 2 ("The Community Meeting in a Psychiatric Hospital: The Experimental Use of a Large Group as Group Psychotherapy") and Appendix 3 ("Family Therapy in Psychiatric Hospital Treatment").

THE PSYCHOTHERAPY OF PSYCHOSES

The psychotherapy of those psychotic patients who, despite their psychoses, are motivated, cooperative, and competent enough to comply with the arrangements for therapy requires no alteration or modification of the therapist's offering as therapy a nondirective relationship of communicative intimacy. However, as in all psychotherapies, the timing and content of responses by the therapist are a matter of clinical judgment and experience. The skillful therapist assesses the patient's tolerance and readiness and then decides when and how much to share of his own inner state and reactions to the patient's behavior.

A problem peculiar to the psychotherapy of psychotic patients is the exquisite sensitivity of paranoid patients to subtle nuances of the therapist's behavior.

Clinical Examples of Sensitivity in Psychosis

1. A young adult schizophrenic male patient observed me opening my office door while one hand was in the pocket of my trousers. He became agitated and accused me of making homosexual advances toward him.
2. A middle-aged paranoid female patient reacted furiously to my offering to shake hands with her at our first meeting in my office, accusing me of attempting to seduce her.

3. A young adult female schizoaffective patient accused me (correctly) of concealing my disgust over hearing her graphic accounts of her passive submission to sadomasochistic abuse by her male "lover."

Doing therapy with ambulatory psychotic patients requires more vigilant self-awareness on the part of the therapist than when treating nonpsychotic patients so as not to provoke paranoid reactions. Scrupulous honesty with the patient is essential to establishing a therapeutic alliance and overcoming the psychotic patient's suspiciousness.

Responding to delusional statements by psychotic patients presents another problem for the psychotherapist. He should be honest. If the therapist is convinced that the patient "really" believes in the reality of his delusions or his hallucinations, then the therapist should confess his own disbelief. If, however, the therapist doubts that the patient "really" believes his own expressed delusions, then he can possibly offer the speculation that the patient seems to be motivated to try to convince the therapist that the patient is functionally deranged and incompetent. The essence of this kind of dialogue with a psychotic patient is that it conveys to the patient that the therapist regards him as being an intact human being as far as his central nervous system is concerned; that the therapist believes the patient is functioning with the same premises for interpersonal behavior as all normal humans; and that the therapist regards the patient's behavior as being motivated, purposeful, goal directed, and understandable once the patient gives up his interest in being obscure, cryptic, incoherent, bizarre, and esoteric.

For purposes of doing effective psychotherapy with psychotics, the therapist should regard the patient's alleged psychosis as being not a matter of having a thought disorder, but rather a matter of having a disorder of motivation, namely, a desire to assume the sick role and be regarded and treated by others as a "psychotic" person for such reasons as secondary gain, avoidance of anxiety-producing responsibilities, or phobic fears of anticipated social stress, intimacy, rejection, and so forth. Psychotic behavior is viewed by the therapist as being a form of malingering derived from early life trauma, deprivation, and retarded psychosocial development. This view of psychosis as motivated behavior is admittedly not in the mainstream of psychiatry as practiced today, but it has been characterized similarly in older psychoanalytic literature (see Frieda Fromm-Reichmann [1950], Stekel [1924]; and later also Brody and Redlich [1954], Rakusin and Fierman [1963], Szasz [1961], and Towbin [1966]; see also description of the so-called Ganser syndrome by Arieti [1959].

However, the concept of psychosis as motivated behavior has appeared in nonclinical literature (see Günter Grass's novel *The Tin Drum* [1959]; Ken Kesey's *One Flew Over the Cuckoo's Nest* [1962]; Pirandello's *Henry IV* [1979]; and Shakespeare's *Hamlet* [1985].

Clinical Examples of Motivation in Psychosis

1. A young adult schizophrenic patient shouted at me, "What do I have to do to prove to you I'm insane, kill someone?"

2. A middle-aged patient, chronically hospitalized in a veterans hospital and receiving a 100 percent service-connected disability pension for schizophrenia, also shouted at me, "I'll prove to you I'm not this way just for

the money or just to stay here! I'm going to return my pension and tell them to stop sending it to me!" I laughed and responded, "I'm pretty sure you know that would only convince them that you must be insane to want to give up all that money!" He then joined me in laughing at his own threat.

3. A teenage schizophrenic patient confessed that when he experienced extreme depression, loneliness, and nostalgia for his friends in the hospital, he would report to his parents that hallucinatory voices were telling him to commit suicide and that he had to be rehospitalized.

Attempting psychotherapy with psychotic patients who threaten or engage in violence can be distracting to the psychotherapist. The therapist should take whatever precautions are necessary to ensure his safety, such as having another person outside or near the office who can be called for assistance. A rule of thumb is always to position oneself between the patient and the door. If threats continue, it might be helpful to say to the patient something like, "I have trouble listening to what you have to say to me if I have to keep thinking of how to defend myself!" Similarly, when confronted by a psychotic patient with escalating anger, it might be helpful to interrupt the patient and to engage in a calm, protracted, rationalizing type of statement until the patient is distracted from his fury.

Attempting psychotherapy with involuntary, committed, or resistant hospitalized psychotic patients can best be done with a therapist/administrator split type of arrangement made with the institution as previously discussed. The therapist can then present himself to the patient as being neutral, uninvolved, unrelated, and disassociated from the personnel responsible for the patient's incarceration, and can offer the patient a confidant relationship of trust and alliance.

If the patient appears delusional, the therapist should avoid taking issue with the delusions until a therapeutic relationship has been established. In dealing with mute or catatonic patients, the therapist should engage in a friendly monologue responding to the body language of the patient or discussing what he knows of the patient's history or life circumstances. If permissible and if the patient is cooperative, the therapist might find walking with the patient either indoors or outdoors during the therapy sessions conducive to breaking through the patient's catatonia and resistance.

Finally, those brave psychotherapists who attempt to treat psychotic patients must resign themselves to a stormy, unpredictable, lengthy, challenging, and sometimes dangerous venture. But the rewards can be gratifying when the patient finally gives up his psychotic maneuvers, accepts the therapist as a confidant, and begins to return to a normal lifestyle free of the fears and torments that drove his past psychotic escapism.

NONDIRECTIVE PSYCHOTHERAPY AS AN ADJUNCTIVE THERAPY

Patients with medical, organic, neurologic, infectious, allergic, or other biochemical disorders are by no means immune to psychoneurotic or so-called functional psychotic disorders as well. Definitive, curative, nondirective psychotherapy can and should be included in the treatment plan for such patients. Even though such patients may be permanently disabled or limited by their physical illnesses, they can and should be able to live free of neurotic symptoms, enjoying as full a psychosocial life as possible and fulfilling their creative potential as much as possible.

To maximize the effectiveness of psychotherapy with such patients, it would be ideal for the psychotherapist not to be personally involved or responsible for the patient's medical, physical, neurological, or pharmacological treatment. Ideally he should not even be responsible for prescribing psychopharmacotherapy for his patients with so-called chemical imbalance or neurotransmitter disorders, that is, mood disorders, anxiety disorders, or psychoses. Again, the rationale for the psychotherapist not to be responsible for his patient's medication is that his egalitarian, nondirective relationship with his patient would be compromised. The reality of the patient's dependency on the therapist for medication would reinforce the patient's fusion-fantasy-based psychological dependency and would interfere with the hoped-for maturizing effects of his psychotherapy.

This point of view is admittedly not in the mainstream of current psychiatric practice. Psychiatrists are taught and trained today to assume full responsibility for their patients, and it is understandable that a modern-day psychotherapist may be convinced that he is "really" responsible for supervising and directing many areas of his patient's life. He may well feel obliged to advise his patient in these areas and to assume responsibility for his patient's medications. Unfortunately, to the extent that he does this he will fail to practice effective psychotherapy. While probably no therapist is perfect, the closer one comes to providing completely nondirective communicative intimacy, the more effective his therapy will be.

However, in these days of managed care it is unlikely that third-party payers or even patients themselves would approve of two psychiatrists, one for psychotherapy and the other for psychopharmacotherapy. Of course, this is not the case when the psychotherapist is not a physician, in which case he can readily refer his patient to a psychiatrist for medication. Psychiatrist psychotherapists attempting nondirective psychotherapy must simply do the best they can, prescribe medications as needed, and try to minimize the negative effects on therapy by sharing with their patients their concerns and their reactions to the patients' fusion behavior.

LEARNING AND TEACHING PSYCHOTHERAPY

Regretfully, psychotherapists today are not usually trained to do open-ended, definitive, nondirective psychotherapy. Psychoanalysts are, of course, trained to do long-term therapy, but their commitment to analytic activity precludes their establishing a truly nondirective relationship with their patients. The promotion and reinforcement of dependent behavior is inherent in the traditional psychoanalytic relationship. Fortunately, many analysts have abandoned the analytic position relative to their patients and do practice effective, nonauthoritarian psychotherapy.

In teaching this brand of psychotherapy it is best for the teacher or supervisor of the student therapist to teach by demonstration, that is, to relate to the student in as nondirective a manner as is practicable within the contractual responsibilities of the teacher. Rather than structure the teaching or supervisory session, the teacher can simply invite the student to feel free to bring up whatever matters he wishes to discuss. The teacher thus offers the student a nondirective relationship of communicative intimacy with the necessary proviso that the teacher will offer advice and direction when necessary in regard to the therapy of the student's patients. To learn and then become committed to this brand of psychotherapy, the student must first find a teacher experienced in it, and then must find it either effective when applied to his own patients or successful in his own personal therapy with a practitioner of this therapy, or both.

The task of learning communicative-intimacy psychotherapy is not an easy one. The student must, in effect, unlearn all the mythological dogmas about psychotherapy that he has been taught before (see Appendix 1: "Myths in the Practice of Psychotherapy"). He must resist the current trend to overemphasize the biological, genetic, and biochemical aspects of behavior and mental illness as well as the sole use of psychotropic drugs as treatment to the exclusion of psychosocial therapies. However, the student will enjoy his newfound skill, once mastered, in providing effective, curative, maturizing, creativity-enhancing psychotherapy for his patients. Not only will he enjoy better results with his psychotherapy patients, he will also find doing communicative-intimacy-promoting therapy more fun, more alive and interesting, less taxing, and less boring than doing his previous traditional psychotherapies.

5

EMPOWERING THE PATIENT TO COPE WITH MANAGED CARE

In all industrialized countries of the world the explosive increase in the costs of providing health care has resulted in a variety of national strategies ranging from unregulated fee-for-service systems to government-controlled health plans. In the United States, systems of health care delivery have included private health insurance, health maintenance organizations (HMOs), Medicare, and Medicaid. Over the past few years a new health insurance industry has emerged known as *managed care,* which purports to provide all necessary care at an affordable price. Indeed, these new managed care companies have been very successful in demonstrating that they can markedly reduce the costs of health care and, as a result, they have been contracted by industry, government, and private and public businesses throughout the country until they now dominate the country's entire health care delivery system.

How do they do it? They do it by drastically using established business methods for controlling and reducing costs and services and eliminating waste. They establish panels of carefully selected health providers who agree to submit to managed care control over their clinical practice. Patients are denied freedom of choice of doctors and must choose from the managed care list of providers. Doctors are denied freedom of choice of patients and must get approval from managed care before the patient's treatment will be covered by insurance. Doctors are told what treatments they can and cannot prescribe, how often and how long they can treat any patient, and who can and cannot be hospitalized. These standards and controls are usually not set by qualified medical experts and specialists but rather by personnel, both clinical and nonclinical, whose driving interest is to cut the costs of medical care and to increase the profits of the managed care insurance companies. Any clinical provider who dares to object to the arbitrary limitations imposed on his patient's treatment is at risk of being summarily "terminated without cause" as a provider and removed from the list of providers available to the managed care insurance company's subscribers.

Managed care extends its influence over the country's health delivery system by relentless lobbying of legislatures and aggressive marketing to industries. The practice of psychotherapy has been especially compromised within the burgeoning managed care insurance industry. Mental health professionals who apply for provider status are frequently rejected if their practice emphasizes psychotherapy rather than psychopharmacotherapy. Even if psychotherapists are accepted as providers by managed care companies, long-term psychotherapy is simply never approved for reimbursement. Short-term psychotherapy is approved if justification is presented by either the patient or the therapist to a managed care official "gatekeeper," but approval is still limited by the company to only a few sessions. The patient's confidentiality is sacrificed when the therapist has to plead his case with managed care gatekeepers. In my own practice, authorization was limited to only six weekly therapy sessions for one of my patients with recurrent severe depression and to only once a month for four months for another patient with a diagnosis of chronic paranoid schizophrenia. In both instances, the patient's therapy had to shift from moving toward healing and liberation to focusing on suppression of symptoms before the insurance ran out. The unregulated managed care industry is actually a managed cost industry that provides minimum care for maximum profit. The inflated salaries of managed care company executives are in the millions and have been publicized nationally.

Psychotherapists dedicated to providing their patients with effective and curative psychotherapy will advise and counsel their patients in order to motivate and empower them to cope with the constraints of their managed care health insurance. To do this the therapist must deviate from his psychotherapeutic relationship as a nonauthoritarian, nondirective confidant whose sole interest is to engage in communicative intimacy with his patient. For the psychotherapist to become an active advisor and advocate for his patient may adversely affect the psychotherapy and may reinforce his patient's dependency and fusion-seeking behavior. Nonetheless, this danger has to be weighed against the greater threat of harsh limitation or even total denial of coverage for the therapy by managed care. The therapist should communicate and share his dilemma fully with the patient. By so doing he may minimize the antitherapeutic effect of his accepting the directive role of advocate and advisor.

The model of psychotherapy presented in this book should be viewed as a generic approach that may be modified in order to cope with the various realities of life circumstances, including managed care. The old quip, "The operation was a success but the patient died," must not be a metaphor for unrealistic adherence to the nonauthoritarian practices of effective psychotherapy. To empower the patient to cope successfully with managed care, the therapist should counsel the patient to the following goals:

1. *Reject the misconceptions of managed care.* Effective psychotherapy motivates patients to make a lifetime commitment to seeking full liberation from neurotic constrictions of their autonomy, independence, and creativity. If this is to be achieved by the patient, it is essential that the therapist, also, must not compromise his own commitment to independence and autonomy. The patient must be empowered by the therapist and the therapy to resist the false implications of managed care, namely, that longer-term psychotherapy is not medically necessary and that his mental health needs can be simply and quickly met by (1) taking psychiatric medication to relieve symptoms, and (2) using short-term counseling or crisis intervention to relieve or solve current social problems. A recent survey by consultants for *Consumer Reports* magazine (1995) showed that psychotherapy was an effective treatment and that people in therapy more than six months reported the most progress.

Patients must understand that the simplistic approach of managed care disregards the vast experience, knowledge, and research about the human mind, psychopathology, and behavior pathology accumulated over the past century by scientists and clinicians from many professional disciplines. It discards all that is known about learning theory, conditioning, reinforcement, child rearing, symptom formation, symptom extinction, and all the other complex social and experiential influences on human development and human behavior. Worst of all, the managed care quick-fix approach leaves the patient vulnerable to future recurrence.

2. *Assess the patient's mental health needs fully.* This is essential for any therapy to be successful, especially if managed care is involved. Psychiatric symptoms are almost always an extension of underlying personality and character psychopathology, which must be addressed and overcome to prevent relapse and recidivism. Managed care has shown little interest in supporting the longer-term psychotherapy needed as a preventative to avoid recurrence of the patient's symptom neurosis.

A person's mental health needs are more than relief of symptoms and improvement of social adjustment. Full mental health also means freedom to exercise one's natural talents and aptitudes, to experience self-actualization (Maslow 1971), and to be an autonomous, independent, and creative human being. A mentally healthy individual is capable of pursuing his self-interests with a minimum of inner constraints, inhibitions, or psychopathological constrictions. Psychopharmacology is not chemical psychotherapy, as claimed by pharmaceutical advertisements. To truly free the human spirit requires long-term psychotherapy (Seligman 1996), not the Band-Aid, patch-up brief encounters authorized by managed care health insurance companies.

From a clinical point of view it may be relatively easy to alleviate psychiatric symptoms, with either psychopharmacology or brief psychotherapy or both. Similarly, it is relatively easy to help patients improve their social adjustment with directive counseling, crisis intervention, or brief cognitive psychotherapy. Managed care supports and approves such brief treatments but does a disservice when it rejects longer-term therapy aimed at curing basic psychopathology, personality disorders, character neuroses, and so forth, and ignores the patient's vulnerability to relapse and recidivism.

3. *Be an advocate for the patient.* Unfortunately, managed care has been able to impose its draconian restrictions on the practice of psychotherapy with a minimum of resistance from organized psychiatry and psychology because of the rapid uncritical acceptance by the health insurance industry, the business and industrial community, and government at all levels, all eager to cut the heavy costs of health care even if it means reducing the quality of care provided.

In our society it is well known that providing mental health care has always had low priority because of stigma, prejudice, and lack of convincing data to support claims for definitive treatment for the mentally ill. What gains were made occurred only after prolonged and persistent lobbying by advocacy groups. Whenever budgetary reductions become necessary, however, support for the treatment of the mentally ill is one of the first of the expenditures to be reduced or even eliminated. Such reductions are frequently falsely rationalized as being done because treatment is ineffective or because the mentally ill are basically incurable. The reduction of federal support for community mental health centers is one such example. The reduction of mental health treatment services in the country's prisons is another. The limitations of psychotherapy imposed by managed care is another.

It is sometimes possible for psychotherapists to plead successfully with managed care companies to extend coverage of psychotherapy for their patients. On several occasions I have been able to persuade a managed care gatekeeper that my patient needed more than the meager number of therapy sessions allotted. Extensions were granted—not enough to meet my patient's needs but better than none.

4. *Identify alternative options when psychotherapy is denied.* When managed care authorization for psychotherapy is denied or curtailed, the therapist should help his patient identify and seek alternatives such as:

Self pay: This is an alternative for those who have access to funds and who are motivated enough to pay for psychotherapy without recourse to health insurance coverage. For those whose access to funds is limited, it may be necessary to search for a therapist willing to reduce the fee if their first therapist does not accommodate them. More and more psychotherapists are reducing their fees in exchange for the freedom from completing endless insurance forms and having to negotiate with third-party payers, including managed care.

Clinics: State-subsidized outpatient mental health centers and clinics are also available, and many have a sliding scale fee policy. The risk, of course, is that the therapists available in such clinics may still be in training, inexperienced, and as yet unable to provide competent effective psychotherapy.

Intermittent therapy: Health insurance policies usually provide their benefits on an annual basis. This means that when the authorization for limited psychotherapy runs out, the patient may reapply the following year for another round of psychotherapy, and may even arrange to alternate periods of reimbursed therapy with periods of self-pay therapy.

Group therapy: Low-cost group therapies may be available to the patient who cannot afford or obtain individual psychotherapy covered by health insurance. Here again, the patient must avoid directive group therapists who promote dependency.

Support groups: No-fee leaderless support groups are also available in many areas of the country. These are usually focused on a single clinical theme: for example, widows, singles, men's or women's groups, and so forth. So-called twelve-step "Anonymous" programs are also widespread, such as, Alcoholics, Narcotics, Overeaters, and Gamblers. Unfortunately, these groups tend to be ritualized and are unlikely to provide psychotherapeutic relationships promoting communicative intimacy. They are effective, however, in helping their members overcome addictions and compulsive behavior.

Psychotherapeutic relationships: Some people, although untrained and unsophisticated, are nonetheless natural-born psychotherapists who are able to provide a nondirective confidant relationship of communicative intimacy to those fortunate enough to come to them for psychotherapeutic help (Towbin 1978). They may be nurses, doctors, clergy, or just simply friendly and helpful neighbors or associates who frequently have a history since childhood of attracting friends who confided to them. Close friends, lovers, family, and relatives may also be able to offer some measure of the nondirective, nonjudgmental, communicative intimacy necessary to have a psychotherapeutic effect.

Meditation practice: Meditation can be an effective form of do-it-yourself psychotherapy. Meditation that emphasizes looking within oneself in a nonjudgmental, noncritical, open way over time can lead to psychological change. Attitudes, values, and memories that restrict and inhibit one's self-esteem, creativity, and spontaneity can be modified by regularly scheduled meditation sessions. It is helpful to discuss the events that occur in one's meditation sessions with a colleague or someone familiar with meditation practice (Dhiravamsa 1990).

While none of the above alternatives to formal psychotherapy is likely to provide the same degree of effectiveness as formal effective psychotherapy, they may contribute to the ongoing progress of the individual seeking liberation from neurotic constraints and inhibitions. Life itself can be psychotherapeutic as individuals are tested in the flame of interactions with others, experiencing successes and failures, gratifications and frustrations, joy and despair, intimacies and rejections.

The harm that managed care has inflicted on the practice of psychotherapy may well be a transitory phenomenon in this country's history of providing mental health care to its citizens. When it becomes more apparent that only the wealthy and privileged are able to obtain needed competent mental health services, the currently unmanaged managed care industry will probably become regulated and legislatively mandated to provide appropriate and full access to effective and curative psychotherapy. Until then, psychotherapists and their patients must do the best they can. As with many problems of life, there may be no single simple solution, but one can always "do something!" and avoid not only the psychologically devastating effect of feeling impotent and helpless but also the equally demoralizing effect of submitting to, or agreeing with, false belief systems. The psychological health of a human being is manifested more in how he maintains his integrity in his struggles against adversity than in whether he succeeds or fails in overcoming the specific problems of life.

Serious psychotherapists confronted with the onslaught of the forces of managed care must strive to keep alive the practice of curative transforming psychotherapy. By offering his full innermost presence to his patient, the therapist becomes the healing force that can bring the patient to a new and better life, free of symptoms, free of neurotic constrictions, free of inhibitions, and free of fear.

REFERENCES

Arieti, S. (1959). Ganser's Syndrome. In *American Handbook of Psychiatry* 1:547–548. New York: Basic Books.
Bowlby, J. (1969). *Attachment.* New York: Basic Books.
Brody, E. B., and Redlich, F. C. (1954). *Psychotherapy with Schizophrenics.* New York: International Universities Press.
Buber, M. (1958). *I and Thou,* trans. R. G. Smith. New York: Charles Scribner and Sons, 1923.
Caplan, R., and Caplan, G. (1969). *Psychiatry and the Community in Nineteenth-Century America: The Recurring Concern with the Environment in the Prevention and Treatment of Mental Illness.* New York: Basic Books.
Dhiravamsa. (1990). *Turning to the Source: An Eastern View of Western Mind Using Insight Meditation and*

Psychotherapy for Personal Growth, Health & Wholeness. Grass Valley, CA: Blue Dolphin Press.

Fierman, L. B., ed. (1965). *Effective Psychotherapy/The Contribution of Hellmuth Kaiser.* New York: Free Press/ Macmillan.

Freud, S. (1905). Fragment of an analysis of a case of hysteria. *Standard Edition* 7:73–122.

——— (1914). On narcissism: an introduction. *Standard Edition* 14:69–104.

——— (1923). The ego and the id. *Standard Edition* 19:3–59.

Fromm-Reichmann, F. (1950). *Principles of Intensive Psychotherapy.* Chicago: University of Chicago Press.

Grass, G. (1959). *The Tin Drum.* New York: Pantheon/ Random House.

Harlow, H. F., and Mears, C. (1979). *The Human Model: Primate Perspectives.* New York: Halsted.

Hebb, D. O. (1949). *The Organization of Behavior: A Neurophysiological Theory.* New York: Wiley.

Jones, E. (1955). *The Life and Work of Sigmund Freud,* vol. 2. New York: Basic Books.

Kaiser, H. (1955). The problem of responsibility in psychotherapy. *Psychiatry* 18:205–211.

——— (1959). Personal communication.

——— (1965a). The universal symptom of the psychoneuroses: a search for the conditions of effective psychotherapy. In *Effective Psychotherapy/The Contribution of Hellmuth Kaiser,* ed. L. B. Fierman, pp. 14–171. New York: Free Press/Macmillan.

——— (1965b). Types of ideation in neurotic patients. In *Effective Psychotherapy,* pp. 131–133.

——— (1965c). The vicious circle. In *Effective Psychotherapy,* pp. 152–154.

Kesey, K. (1962). *One Flew Over the Cuckoo's Nest.* New York: Viking.

Kierkegaard, S. (1844). *The Concept of Dread.* Princeton: Princeton University Press.

Lowen, A. (1958). *Physical Dynamics of Character Structure*. New York: Grune & Stratton.

Maslow, A. H. (1971). *The Farther Reaches of Human Nature*. New York: Viking.

——— (1995). Mental health: Does therapy help? *Consumer Reports*, November, pp. 734–738.

Piaget, J. (1952). *The Origins of Intelligence in Children*, trans. M. Cook. New York: International Universities Press.

Pirandello (1979). *Henry IV*, trans. J. Mitchell. London: Byre Methuen.

Rakusin, J. M., and Fierman, L. B. (1963). Five assumptions for treating chronic psychotics. *Mental Hospital* 14:140–148.

Rogers, C. R. (1961). *On Becoming A Person.* Boston: Houghton Mifflin.

Rolf, I. (1963). Structural Integration. *Systematics* 1:1.

Seligman, M. E. P. (1996). The pitfalls of managed care. *The Independent Practitioner* 16:73–75.

Shakespeare, W. (1985). *Hamlet, Prince of Denmark*, ed. E. Philip. Cambridge: Cambridge University Press.

Spitz, R. A. (1965). *The First Year of Life: A Psychoanalytic Study of Normal and Deviant Development of Object Relations*. New York: International Universities Press.

Stekel, W. (1924). *Peculiarities of Behavior*, trans. J. S. Van Teslar. New York: Boni and Liveright.

Szasz, T. (1961). *The Myth of Mental Illness*. New York: Harper and Row.

Towbin, A. P. (1966). Understanding the mentally deranged. *Journal of Existentialism* 7:63–68.

——— (1978). The confiding relationship: a new paradigm. *Psychotherapy: Theory, Research and Practice* 15:333–343.

Appendix 1

MYTHS IN THE PRACTICE OF PSYCHOTHERAPY[1]

[1]Copyright © 1965 by the American Medical Association. Reprinted from *Archives of General Psychiatry* 12, April, 408–414. Used with permission.

The practice of clinical medicine has been subject throughout its history to the influences of clinical myths. These myths consist of clinical principles and practices that although seemingly rational at their inception, even proven "true" according to existent criteria, nevertheless were proven subsequently in the test of time and clinical experience to be worthless or even harmful (Major 1954, Zilboorg and Henry 1941).

Clinical psychiatry seems even more than other specialties to be vulnerable to the formation of clinical myths due to vexing problems of control and validation in psychiatric research. These myths take the form of unproven assertions about practice that erroneously have become regarded as clinical facts. They are, essentially, empirical propositions never put to the test (Wheelis 1958). At least once each decade psychiatry should reexamine its premises, theories, and practices to decide which to retain and which to discard. Particularly insidious are those myths that justify not treating whole classes of patients psychotherapeutically and those that promote harmful or ineffectual treatments.

Clinical myths in the practice of psychotherapy have to do with the prerequisites, requirements, and conditions necessary for successful and effective psychotherapy: first, in regard to the patient; second, on the part of the therapist; and finally, in regard to the conduct and process of therapy.

THE PATIENT

First, in regard to the patient, the following mythical preconditions are frequently insisted upon by therapists before the patient is regarded as acceptable for psychotherapy.

1. *Nonpsychotic* (Aarons 1962, Glover 1954): *Psychotics are not amenable to psychotherapy.* Freud contributed to this attitude in his writings, although many of the patients whom he regarded as being psychoneurotic and treatable psychoanalytically would now be diagnosed as borderline psychotic or ambulatory schizophrenic. Many psychotherapists in training institutions, clinics, and private practice attest to the value and effectiveness of psychotherapy for communicative psychotics (Brody and Redlich 1954, Burton 1961, Bychowski 1952, Fromm-Reichmann 1950, Weinstein 1962). Even with chronically ill and "back-

ward" psychotics, psychotherapy when attempted has proven helpful and valuable (Rakusin and Fierman 1963). Even in the field of organic psychosis and mental retardation, reports on the value of psychotherapeutic approaches are increasing (Eisenberg and Sharpe 1964, Masland et al. 1948). Similarly, reports of psychotherapy on psychopaths and patients with character disorders all claim good response to sustained competent psychotherapy (Hoeck-Gradenweitz 1963, Karpman 1947, Schmiedeberg 1962).

2. *Age* (Diethelm 1955, Glover 1954, Hollingshead and Redlich 1958): The elderly are still being excluded as being too old, but geriatric psychotherapy has become more accepted by clinicians and is increasingly being reported as successful and effective (Simon and Engle 1964).

3. *Social Class* (Brill and Storrow 1969, Hollingshead and Redlich 1958): *The lower social classes are not treatable psychotherapeutically*. This myth is refuted by the fact that in many clinical training programs in state and federal hospitals and clinics (Weinstein 1962), psychotherapy has been used for years on patients from lower social classes with results that range from fair to good (Brown and Kosterlitz 1964). It is likely that results would be even better if the training experience and competence of the therapists in these settings were better. It is no coincidence that this myth serves to justify the prejudice that all too often exists among clinicians in regard to treating patients of different social classes, societies, or cultures. Needed research in techniques of overcoming crosscultural communication barriers is impeded by this myth and prejudice. This myth is part of the general tendency of uncritical psychotherapists to characterize their own limitations

in doing psychotherapy as being patient qualities that indicate poor prognosis.

4. *Motivation* (Aarons 1962, Diethelm 1955, Glover 1958, Sullivan 1956): The clinical myth that the patient must be motivated for psychotherapy dies hard. Clinicians dealing psychotherapeutically with children, psychotics, character disorders, involuntary and committed patients, in all of whom stated motivation by the patient is obviously absent, know how meaningless the requirement is that the patient must pledge allegiance to Freud, psychiatry, and psychotherapy in order to be treated psychotherapeutically. Committed patients, involuntary patients, unwilling patients, uncooperative patients, all have been and are being treated psychotherapeutically and effectively (Allen 1942, Fromm-Reichmann 1950, Kaiser 1955, Patterson et al. 1962, Schmiedeberg 1962).

5. *Psychological-Mindedness* (Aarons 1962, Hollingshead and Redlich 1958): This mythical requirement, like those regarding motivation and social class, has become part of the lore of psychotherapeutic psychiatry. It was produced in part by the class arrogance that characterized many psychiatrists of the past and, unfortunately, some of the present. Another factor leading to this mythical requirement is that professional defensiveness that finds comfort and security in blaming therapeutic failure on the characteristics of alleged inferiority in the patient. Proof that these requirements are mythical can be found in any clinical facility where patients without these alleged requirements are being treated with psychotherapy with results not significantly different than with those patients endowed with the mythical prerequisites of upper-social class, motivation, and psychological-mindedness.

6. *Intelligence* (Diethelm 1955, Hollingshead and Redlich 1958): New interest and efforts by clinicians with retarded, feebleminded, and organically impaired patients give hope to the application of psychotherapy to this formerly neglected group of patients (Eisenberg and Sharpe 1964, Masland et al. 1948) heretofore excluded from psychotherapeutic treatment on theoretical grounds.

7. *Education* (Gurin et al. 1960): This mythical prerequisite for successful psychotherapy is usually not given as a separate prerequisite but appears as a factor in determining the presence of other alleged necessary conditions, such as social class, but as with the other preconditions, it is simply not borne out by clinical trial (Brown and Kosterlitz 1964).

In summary, in regard to the selection of patients for psychotherapy, the prerequisite conditions of nonpsychotic diagnosis, proper age, upper social class, motivation, psychological-mindedness, intelligence, and education are mythical and not verifiable clinically. However, the questions remain as to what part, if any, these conditions play in the conduct, process, and outcome of psychotherapy; and, second, what the necessary preconditions are for the selection of patients for psychotherapy.

Psychotherapy is a nonorganic, nonphysical, nonpharmacological treatment aimed at influencing, modifying, or removing undesirable aspects of the patient's personality, reactions, and behavior patterns. The medium of psychotherapy is the communicative behavior of the therapist, and it requires only the physical presence of the patient, and that he be at least potentially available in a neurophysiological sense to receive the therapist's communications (Enelow

1960, Kaiser 1955). The patient's psychopathology and behavior pathology represent the sum total of his previous learning and conditioning, and are entirely determined and motivated. Fortunately the patient can be influenced by new learning and new conditioning, which is, of course, the function of psychotherapy. The patient's resistance to change, his rigidity, and his tenacious hold on his own pathology determine the quality and quantity of the forces opposing the efforts or, at least, the intentions of the psychotherapist. This quality of rigidity is therefore the essence of the clinical problem against which the psychotherapist is engaged. If he is successful, the rigidity of the patient's thinking and behavior gives way to flexibility and a change in the direction of psychological maturity and health (Rogers 1961). Thus, factors that contribute to the rigidity of the patient's psychological organization will make the patient in a sense more severely ill and more difficult to treat successfully, and may even possibly make him untreatable, but only in the sense that a massive bacterial infection might not respond to antibiotic treatment while the same infection of lesser intensity might well respond to the same antibiotic treatment. Thus, conceivably, a dull depressed patient might be more rigid and unresponsive in therapy than a bright depressed patient. Yet, conceivably, a dull obsessive-compulsive patient might be less rigid than a bright obsessive-compulsive patient in psychotherapy, and thus more responsive to treatment. So, while age, intelligence, social class, and even possibly motivation and psychological-mindedness might be related or even correlated with the patient's psychological rigidity, and, in a sense, might be indices of the severity of the patient's psychological disorder, nonetheless they do not contraindicate the clinical trial of psychotherapy. Nor do they permit sharp prognoses of success or failure, but only indicate in a general way the probable difficulties in the clinical course and response to therapy. Even this prediction cannot be made on these factors with any probability that would differ significantly from chance, because the outcome of therapy is related to many uncontrollable variables in addition to the patient's own rigidity.

Now to the question of what, if any, are the necessary preconditions for psychotherapy on the part of the patient. There are two: first, that the patient be physically available for psychotherapy sessions, even if on an involuntary basis, and, second, that the patient be psychologically available for meaningful communicative interaction with the therapist. That is to say the obvious, that psychotherapy may not occur if the patient is absent, in a coma, organically impaired to the point of incompetence, or disoriented by drugs, toxins, or intense persistent emotionality, such as occurs in extreme and persistent psychomotor agitation. Even for these clinical states, patients with these conditions need be excluded from psychotherapy only for the duration of the period of communicative inaccessibility.

There are other commonsense conditions that might also apply to the patient's eligibility for psychotherapy, such as language requirements and the absence of distracting or painful physical illnesses. In short, only the presence of a patient with at least the potential capacity for psychological and communicative interaction with the psychotherapist is required for psychotherapy as far as the patient's requirements are concerned (Enelow 1960, Enelow and Adler 1965, Kaiser 1955, 1962).

THE PSYCHOTHERAPIST

Next, in regard to mythical requirements for a psychotherapist to be a psychotherapist, these have mainly to do with training.

1. *Medical Training: Premedical and medical school training, internship, and psychiatric residency are necessary prerequisites for psychotherapists.* This myth is patently untrue as manifested by the prominence of lay analysts and lay psychotherapists throughout the history of dynamic, analytic, and psychotherapeutic psychiatry. As is well known, this is an interdisciplinary issue that has become inflammatory, with interprofessional war flaring up from time to time between organized psychiatry and psychology over issues of private practice, supervised practice, certification, and licensure. However, no justification can be found for the psychiatric profession insisting that other professional disciplines maintain and define standards of training, qualification, and competence higher and more explicit than its own. The opposition of psychiatrists to the practice of psychotherapy by trained clinical psychologists, for instance, is particularly socially irresponsible in view of the critical manpower shortage in the field of mental illness (Joint Commission on Mental Illness and Health 1961). Many clinicians suggest that psychotherapists of the future will be trained neither in medical schools nor in graduate schools of psychology, but rather in specialized professional schools incorporating the relevant aspects of medical and behavioral sciences. The principle of training will be similar to that involved in the specialized training of dentists, incorporating medical training but on a revised and selected basis. No

one can seriously argue that psychotherapy can be or should be defined as exclusively medical practice.

2. *Psychoanalysis* (Freud 1953, Strupp 1959): *Psychoanalysis is a necessary prerequisite for a psychotherapist.* While this myth is not as widespread as the one regarding medical and psychiatric training for psychotherapists, it is still espoused by many psychoanalysts. Implicit in this contention is that the prospective psychotherapist should be treated as well as trained, and that his own neuroses should be removed as prerequisite to his treating others, either as part of his training analysis or as part of a therapeutic analysis or psychotherapy arranged specifically for this purpose. This clinical myth places a heavy and unnecessary burden on young residents and trainees who, under its influence, make great sacrifices to finance an analysis or therapy that they can ill afford and, as far as their mental health or their professional competence is concerned, is hardly necessary. Conversely, many competent psychotherapists who for one reason or another have never undergone psychoanalysis or psychotherapy needlessly suffer from a sense of inadequacy or inferiority relative to their more analyzed, although not necessarily more competent, colleagues. Of course, this is not to ignore the substantial rewards in terms of prestige and status that may accrue from complying with this mythical requirement.

Related to this myth, but possibly more worthy of serious consideration, is the contention that a necessary prerequisite for a psychotherapist be that he is psychologically healthy and free of neurotic symptoms in order to do psychotherapy. This contention is at best a relative one because few psychotherapists could qualify as paragons of psychological health and maturity. The question then remains, what are the necessary conditions and requirements for a psychotherapist?

There are three essential requirements: (1) that he know how to do psychotherapy, that is to say, that he has had adequate supervised training and clinical experience actually doing therapy; (2) that he be endowed with sensitivity to receive and appreciate the nuances and subtleties of interpersonal communication, particularly of the indirect, covert sort of communication engaged in by psychologically disordered people; and (3) that the therapist be sufficiently free from neurotic difficulties and pedagogic preoccupations with theories and stratagems so as to be able to interact with and respond to his patients in a therapeutically communicative manner.

Of course, if it is true that these are the only requirements of a psychotherapist, then the related questions of what professional disciplines and what professional training are required become even more thorny because competence as a psychotherapist can obviously be achieved via several professional disciplines: medicine, psychology, social work, and pastoral counseling. Yet, this problem will not be solved by making fallacious claims as to the necessity that any one particular discipline be prerequisite to functioning as a psychotherapist. Of course, there is danger on the other hand that a naive and cynical attitude may be adopted by people in the mental health field, namely, that "anyone can do it." Such an attitude will only lower the standards of professionalism already in danger in the field of psychotherapy. For example, that federal funds should be used to demonstrate that housewives can be trained to do psychotherapy (Pines 1962) is fatuous and offensive to psychotherapists. Intelligent housewives can be trained to do most anything including clinical research, automobile repair, flower arranging, tracheotomies, and psychotherapy, and this fact is irrelevant to the need for professional training in the entire field of clinical practice including that of psychotherapy. Professionalism of any sort involves more than technical competence in a limited treatment modality. It requires scholarship, erudition, diagnostic acumen, research orientation, historical sophistication, and, above all else, an implacable sense of ethics and responsibility consistent with the traditions and standards of the particular profession.

CONDUCT AND PROCESS

Finally, some mythical conditions are still frequently cited as necessary for the conduct and process of successful psychotherapy.

1. *Fee* (Braatoy 1954, Kubie 1950): The condition frequently stated that the patient must sacrifice money or its equivalent in order to be successfully treated is a viewpoint more commonly held by private practitioners of psychotherapy and psychoanalysis for obvious reasons. It is one of the more blatant rationalizations used by therapists to justify their own personal needs, desires, or demands relative to their patients. The condition is nonsensical.

2. *Physical Position*: Requirements in regard to the position of the patient are no longer rigidly maintained, other than by a few psychoanalysts, namely, that the patient lie on a couch and free-associate, with care taken that he not face the analyst. The rationale that the couch promotes desirable regression and the claim that it is an empirically useful arrangement remain unproven.

3. *History Taking and Psychological Testing*: Many therapists seem to regard psychotherapy as being a sort of computer-like data-handling situation that requires the patient to provide the therapist with material, history, or other data for its operation. This clinical myth is part of the outmoded concept that psychotherapy is an intellectual learning experience in which the patient exchanges psychological and biographical information in regard to his psychological disorder for the therapist's interpretations, clarifications, formulations, and theoretical abstractions about the workings of his inner mental life and how it got that way in the first place. Psychotherapy does not require that the patient provide historical data or learn how to account for himself either in the past, present, or future in metapsychological terms (Rioch 1954). Psychological testing as a prerequisite to psychotherapy is also mythical, although some therapists may find it, as well as history taking, useful in conceptualizing their patients, but essential to the therapy it is not.

4. *Insight* (Grinker 1961): As every experienced therapist knows, some patients change in therapy without achieving insight and some patients achieve insight without ever changing. In addition, the non-insight-oriented psychotherapies have their cures as well as insight-oriented therapies. The dictum that insight is prerequisite to cure is plainly mythical. Indeed, insight-oriented therapies frequently foster intellectualization, rationalization, dependency, and immaturity in their patients. This follows from the implicit connotations of the relationship existent in insight-oriented therapies, namely, that the patient suffers from ignorance about his own life, and that the therapist by virtue of his superior knowledge, insights, and awareness will cure him via a pedagogic learning experience. The

relationship is inherently hierarchical and authoritarian despite the benevolence of the therapist's manner. This relationship impedes the maturating effects of the therapy.

5. *Frequency* (Thompson 1950): That psychotherapy requires a fixed frequency of sessions is obviously mythical as the widespread variations in frequency occurring in clinical practice indicate. Even the general principle, "the more the merrier," seems not to hold, for some individual patients seem to do better with fewer rather than with more frequent appointments. The entire question of optimum frequency for psychotherapy would seem to be a function of individual needs of the patient and individual style of the therapist. The same could be said for the 50-minute hour.

6. *Duration* (Myers and Auld 1955): The necessity that psychotherapy last for years in order to achieve changes in the basic character structure of the patient seems empirically valid, but here also individual differences have such a wide range that the practice of insisting in advance on a two- or three-year commitment from a patient before agreeing to treat him would seem to be based more on myth than on clinical reality.

What then can be said about the conditions necessary for effective psychotherapy? For myself and others (Enelow 1960, Kaiser 1955, Rogers 1961), they are simply that therapeutic contact be maintained by the therapist with his patient in therapy hours held as frequently as is practicable, over an empirically long enough period of time. Nothing else is then required other than that the therapist engage his patient in as open, direct, spontaneous, and genuine communicative relationship as he can. This is the only necessary and sufficient condition for successful psychotherapy to occur. The simplicity of this clinical model of therapy does not preclude the necessity for prolonged and rigorous training for psychotherapists. Professionalism, clinical responsibility, and clinical competence are not easily or quickly achieved.

There are some miscellaneous myths specifically related not to psychotherapy but rather to clinical psychiatry in general. These myths are espoused by the public at large about psychiatric matters despite mental health education programs sponsored by organized medicine, psychiatry, mental health associations, government health departments, and schools. Still these myths persist and are familiar to us all: "Patients with mental illness are incurable, should not marry, should not bear children, should not drive, should not hold responsible jobs, suffer from defective transmittable heredity, belong in hospitals," and so forth.

Some of these mythical beliefs can be detected even among professional personnel responsible for the care of mentally ill patients including, unfortunately, psychiatrists, psychologists, social workers, nurses, and aides. An example of faulty thinking common in both lay and professional personnel is the mythical attitude toward hospital treatment.

THE HOSPITAL

1. *Hospitals Are Bad for Mental Patients*: This Semmelweis-like attitude can be found in high places, even among clinicians in medical schools and residency training institutions (Talbot et al. 1964). Whatever truth there may

be in the notion that the environment of the patient not only causes but maintains his illness is distorted beyond reason in making the emphasis of a patient's clinical experience one of either keeping him out of or maneuvering him out of a hospital.

2. *Hospitals Are Good for Mental Patients*: Similarly untenable is this mythical notion held by a minority of clinicians that hospitalization in itself will cure the patient by removing him from his noxious environment and providing him with a healthier one, namely, the hospital environment.

These attitudes toward hospitalization possibly would have some merit as subsidiary aspects of a specific treatment program consisting of psychotherapy, drugs, and other organic therapies. As a main treatment modality, however, the long-term benefits of hospital experience are mythical as are the alleged effects of a program concerned solely with preventing or shortening hospitalization. Another myth related to hospitalization has to do with the dilution of the concept of psychotherapy by the specious proposition that everything and anything that happens to a hospitalized psychiatric patient is or should be regarded as therapy. The concepts of milieu therapy (Rioch and Stanton 1953, Stanton and Schwartz 1954) and therapeutic community (Caudill 1958, Jones 1953) are distorted and diluted in conceptualizing all the conditions and activities of the patient as being part of the "therapy." Thus, his hobbies, recreations, vocations, avocations, habits of socializing, idleness, and business all are inappropriately regarded as being or not being "therapeutic." Patients' behavior should not be conceptualized in terms of being therapeutic or not because this only confuses the issue of the responsibility of the clinical staff to provide therapeutic experiences for the patient.

A last category of myths relating to clinical psychiatry in general is in regard to fallacious criteria often used to evaluate mental illness and the results of clinical treatment. These criteria could be called the "trappings of mental health": if the patient is working rather than unemployed, if he is living at home rather than in a hospital, if he is in a hospital for a short time rather than a long time, if he is on an open ward rather than a locked ward, if he is sexually active rather than abstinent, and if he is gregarious rather than seclusive, then he will be regarded by both laymen and professionals as being healthier psychologically than if he were otherwise. Furthermore, if the patient experienced or was experiencing some kind of treatment at the time that he shifted in one or more of these directions, then his therapy would be regarded as effective. Conversely, if no shift or if a reverse shift occurred, then his therapy would be regarded as ineffectual and a failure. In other words, the criterion of social adjustment has been so elevated to a prominence by misguided laymen and clinicians in regard to their conceptualization of mental health and effective psychiatric treatment as to reach the proportions of a clinical myth. Mental health and the effectiveness of psychotherapeutic treatment are not to be determined solely by the criteria of social adjustment (Sargent 1958). The social adjustment of the patient is an index of his mental health only in the context of his maturity, autonomy, freedom from neurotic or psychotic symptoms and character pathology, and the fullest use of his own individual endowment. Social adjustment that relies on infantile props, drugs, or dependent relationships for its maintenance is not a valid sign of either mental health or effective psychotherapy.

REFERENCES

Aarons, A. Z. (1962). Analysis and problems of analyzability. *Psychoanalytic Quarterly* 31:514–531.

Allen, F. H. (1942). *Psychotherapy with Children*. New York: Norton.

Braatoy, T. F. (1954). *Fundamentals of Psychoanalytic Technique*. New York: Wiley.

Brill, N. Q., and Storrow, H. A. (1969). Social class and psychiatric treatment. *Archives of General Psychiatry* 3:340–344.

Brody, E. B., and Redlich, F. C. (1954). *Psychotherapy with Schizophrenics*. New York: International Universities Press.

Brown, J. S., and Kosterlitz, N. (1964). Selection and treatment of psychiatric outpatients. *Archives of General Psychiatry* 11:425–438.

Burton, A. (1961). *Psychotherapy of Psychoses*. New York: Basic Books.

Bychowski, G. (1952). *Psychotherapy of Psychosis*. New York: Grune & Stratton.

Caudill, W. A. (1958). *The Psychiatric Hospital as a Small Society*. Cambridge: Harvard University Press.

Diethelm, O. (1955). *Treatment in Psychiatry*. Springfield, IL: Charles C Thomas.

Eisenberg, L., and Sharpe, L. (1964). Child psychiatry: mental deficiency. *American Journal of Psychiatry* 120:650.

Enelow, A. J. (1960). Silent patient. *Psychiatry* 23:153–158.

Enelow, A. J., and Adler, L. McK. (1965). *What is required of the patient in psychotherapy*? Unpublished data.

Freud, S. (1953). Future prospects of psychoanalytic therapy. In *Collected Papers*, vol. 2, pp. 289–296. London: Hogarth.

Fromm-Reichmann, F. (1950). *Principles of Intensive Psychotherapy*. Chicago: University of Chicago Press.

Glover, E. (1954). Indications of psychoanalysis. *Journal of Mental Science* 100:393–401.

——— (1958). *Technique of Psychoanalysis*. New York: International Universities Press.

Grinker, R. R., Jr. (1961). Ego, insight, and willpower. *Archives of General Psychiatry* 5:91–102.

Gurin, G., Veroff, J., and Feld, S. (1960). *Americans View Their Mental Health*. New York: Basic Books.

Hoeck-Gradenweitz, E. (1963). Treatment of psychopaths in penal institutions. *Psychologie Rundschau* 14:93–114.

Hollingshead, A., and Redlich, F. C. (1958). *Social Class and Mental Illness*. New York: Wiley.

Joint Commission on Mental Illness and Health (1961). *Action for Mental Health*. New York: Science Editions.

Jones, M. (1953). *The Therapeutic Community*. New York: Basic Books.

Kaiser, H. (1955). The problem of responsibility in psychotherapy. *Psychiatry* 18:205–211.

——— (1962). Emergency. *Psychiatry* 25:97–118.

Karpman, B. (1947). *Case Studies of Psychopathology of Crime*. Washington, DC: Medical Science.

Kubie, L. S. (1950). *Practical and Theoretical Aspects of Psychoanalysis*. New York: International Universities Press.

Major, R. H. (1954). *History of Medicine*. Springfield, IL: Charles C Thomas.

Masland, R. L., Sarason, S. B., and Gladwin, T. (1948). *Mental Subnormality: Biological, Psychological and Cultural Factors*. New York: Basic Books.

Myers, J. K., and Auld, F. (1955). Some variables related

to outcome of psychotherapy. *Journal of Clinical Psychology* 11:51–54.

Patterson, V., Harris, R. M., and Bewley, W. (1962). Captive outpatients: program for parolees. In *Current Psychiatric Therapies*, vol. 2, ed. J. H. Masserman, pp. 184–191. New York: Grune & Stratton.

Pines, M. (1962). Training housewives as psychotherapists. *Harper's Magazine* 234:37–42.

Rakusin, J. M., and Fierman, L. B. (1963). Five assumptions for treating chronic psychotics. *Mental Hospital* 14:140–148.

Rioch, D. M., and Stanton, A. H. (1953). Milieu therapy. *Psychiatric Treatment* 21: 94–105.

Rioch, J. (1953). Transference phenomenon in psychoanalytic therapy. *Psychiatry* 6:147–156.

Rogers, C. R. (1961). *On Becoming a Person*. Boston: Houghton Mifflin.

Sargent, H. (1958). Situational variables in psychotherapy: research project of Menninger Foundation—Second Report. *Bulletin of the Menninger Clinic* 4:148–166.

Schmiedeberg, M. (1962). Treatment of psychopaths. In *Current Psychiatric Therapies*, vol. 2, ed. J. H. Masserman, pp. 180–183. New York: Grune & Stratton.

Simon, A., and Engle, B. (1964). Geriatrics (Review of Psychiatric Progress) 1963. *American Journal of Psychiatry* 120:671.

Stanton, A. H., and Schwartz, M. S. (1954). *Mental Hospital*. New York: Basic Books.

Strupp, H. (1959). Toward analysis of therapists' contribution to treatment process. *Psychiatry* 22:349– 362.

Sullivan, H. S. (1956). *Clinical Studies of Psychiatry*. New York: Norton.

Talbot, S., Miller, S. C., and White, R. B. (1964). Some

antitherapeutic side effects of hospitalization and psychotherapy. *Psychiatry* 27:170–176.

Weinstein, G. (1962). Survey of outpatient individual psychotherapy. *Archives of General Psychiatry* 7:21–24.

Wheelis, A. (1958). Vocational hazards of psychoanalysis. In *Quest for Identity.* New York: Norton.

Zilboorg, G., and Henry, G. W. (1941). *History of Medical Psychology.* New York: Norton.

Appendix 2

THE COMMUNITY MEETING IN A PSYCHIATRIC HOSPITAL: THE EXPERIMENTAL USE OF A LARGE GROUP AS GROUP PSYCHOTHERAPY[1]

The inclusion in psychiatric hospital practice of a therapeutic community program modeled after the work of Caudill (1958), Edelson (1970), Fairweather (1969), Jones (1953), Rioch (1953), and others has become commonplace. Therapeutic community programs usually include regularly scheduled community meetings attended by all or most patients in the hospital-at-large, or from designated units, and by all or part of the clinical, nursing, administrative, and management staffs of the hospital or unit. These institutional events are large group meetings subject to large group dynamics. Conventionally, they are conducted as task-oriented work groups concerned with identification, clarification, and resolution of clinical and administrative problems existent in the hospital.

The author had participated in several Tavistock model group relations training conferences involving large study group exercises. He had observed that in these experiential conferences the large group behavior engendered by the nondirective task "to study large group behavior as it occurs" consistently produced among its participants spontaneous communicative interaction, intense emotional impact, "unfreezing" of stereotyped role behavior, and other dramatic behavioral changes. He postulated that community meetings in a psychiatric hospital conducted nondirectively along similar bases as large study group exercises over a sufficient period of time would constitute an effective group psychotherapy experience.

As newly appointed (1971) medical director of a private psychiatric hospital (Elmcrest Psychiatric Institute, Portland, Connecticut) with fifty-two beds in 1971, expanded to 105 beds in 1974, he introduced an intensive therapeutic community program into the hospital. The program included a weekly one-hour community meeting for all patients and staff, which he designated as a large group psychotherapy meeting rather than as a work or business meeting. The primary task of this community meeting continues to be identified to patients and staff as group psychotherapy, but the meetings are conducted, more or less, as a large study group exercise might be, with staff serving collectively as therapists-consultants to the large study group. Staff interventions are offered in the spirit of sharing reactions and observations rather than as interpretations or pedagogy. The content of staff remarks frequently takes the form of group process interpretations as well as revelations of personal affective or cognitive reactions, observations, and associations. Over the years since 1971 the author's hypothesis has been confirmed experientially, namely, that phenomena characteristic of large study group exercises in group relations training conferences do consistently occur in the large group psychotherapy/community meetings of the hospital. In addition, while chaotic, disruptive, aggressive, or hostile behaviors frequently occur, persistent counter-themes of humanistic concern, rescue and support operations, and caring and nurturing behavior characteristic of effective group psychotherapy also frequently occur. Patients participating in the weekly community meeting over periods of weeks and months seem to experience growing trust and openness, excitement and risk taking, counterphobic behavior, and positive feedback, all consistent with group psychotherapy phenomena. The experiences in the community meeting frequently are integrated afterward by the patients with other experiences received in their small group and family therapies during the rest of the hospital treatment program. Finally, impressionistic reports and a questionnaire survey also support the contention that the community meeting constitutes an effective large group psychotherapy.

The proposition that a large group meeting conducted along these lines would provide an effective psychotherapy is not dealt with extensively in the literature. Freud's original article on group psychology (1921) emphasized the importance of identification with the leader. Freud referred to previous studies by LeBon on the psychology of crowds. LeBon had made the point that the behavior of people in large groups simulates that of primitive peoples and children. American clinicians who developed modern concepts of group dynamics and therapy included Burrow (1927), Lewin (1935), Moreno (1958), Schilder (1938), Slavson (1947, 1956), and others. British contributions came from Bion (1959), Ezriel (1950), Foulkes (1964), and others. Rapoport (1960) wrote on the use of community meetings in psychiatric hospitals for social control. Rice and Turquet began large group study exercises in 1957, and described them in their book *Learning for Leadership* (1965). A study by Curry (1967) concluded that psychotherapy could not occur satisfactorily in a large group situation. However, Kreeger (1975), in his book *The Large Group: Dynamics and Therapy,* observed that the large group can be enormously stimulating and provocative of real creative, original thought and that in all hospitals or institutions that try to function as therapeutic communities the large group or community meeting is a sine qua non of the culture. He also observed that in large group experiences psychotic mechanisms abound, and people reported that just the experience of being in a large group puts them more clearly in touch with the primitive aspects of their own personality than any other therapy situation. Furthermore, participating in a large group can add significantly to fuller understanding of oneself and in turn to an increased awareness of personality development and definition of individual psychopathology.

Turquet (1975) described the threat to personal identity experienced by individuals in large group situations. Edelson (1970) firmly espoused the position that psychotherapy was not possible in large groups. However, he did advocate that "sociotherapy" was possible, defining psychotherapy as dealing with problems and tensions between and within individuals, and sociotherapy as dealing with intra- and inter-group tensions. Kreeger (1975) and others have differed with him and charged that his definitions are too rigid, and that the experience and outcome of large group clinical meetings support the contention that a large group psychotherapy is possible and effective.

Carl Rogers (1977) reported on "person-centered" group therapy with a group of over 600 people during a one-week workshop. Most of the week was spent in this unstructured huge encounter group. He did this in the spirit of trial and experiment, and his description of the events parallels our own experience with our weekly community meetings attended by over 120 patients and staff. Rogers identified various phases in his large group therapy: chaotic beginning, gradual development of group cohesiveness, growing humanistic concern between members, and, finally, by the time the week was over, a cohesive and established therapy group with very poignant interchanges between participants in that setting.

At Elmcrest patients and staff participated in a questionnaire evaluation of the weekly one-hour community meetings. The study was designed to assess staff and patient reactions to, and judgments of, the community meeting as a form of group psychotherapy, and to identify some of the variables affecting those reactions, such as length of staff employment and patients' length of stay, staff's professional discipline or department, and previous Tavistock group relations training. Written opinions and recommendations concerning the community meeting were also solicited for study (Minear 1979).

The results of the questionnaire evaluation indicate general agreement (65 percent) among the professional staff that the weekly community meeting does qualify as an effective group psychotherapy. Thirty-five percent of the staff rated its effects as either neutral or harmful. Patients were about evenly divided in this judgment. Neither length of employment at Elmcrest nor professional department or discipline proved significant in determining this judgment. There was, however, a significant positive relationship between having had previous Tavistock group relations training and the more favorable ratings. A patient's length of stay also was found not to be related to a patient's ratings of how the community meeting contributed to his treatment experience.

Several major themes favorable to the community meeting appeared in the staff's narrative responses on the questionnaire. Using such terms as "barometer," "pulse," "atmosphere," and "emotional climate," staff members reported obtaining a useful sense of the attitudinal disposition of patients in the hospital-at-large through observing interactions between the various subgroups in the meetings. A sense of community and family was reported. The meetings provided opportunities for self-expression and self-exploration, inter- and intra-unit confrontations, and sharing and receiving helpful feedback. The community meeting was acknowledged as an opportunity to learn about one's own reactions to anxiety-producing situations. Others commented on enjoying the frequent humorous and entertaining experiences occurring in the meetings. The community meeting also was appreciated as a "gathering of the clan," providing a sense of family, community, and continuity. Staff members reported enjoying the weekly encounter with colleagues, fellow clinicians, new employees, and old and new patients of the hospital.

Prevalent criticisms of the community meeting were its nondirectiveness, lack of structure and organization, and occasional lack of control with resulting group chaos, fragmentation, negativism, and threats of violence. Some staff complained of high anxiety resulting from the "intense, disorganized, emotional experience, usually with lack of closure." Some experienced concern over the fear of escalating acting-out behavior. Some complained that the meeting occasionally became "an arena for inter-staff political chicanery, egotistical exhibitionism, and attempts to confuse, frighten, and mislead patients." Others expressed dissatisfaction with the community meeting as fostering post-meeting chaos, disorder, and disruption in patients, and producing feelings of tension and anxiety in staff.

A pervasive positive theme expressed by patients was that the community meeting brought together the entire hospital community and offered a chance to meet and give and receive feedback from one another. Patients commented that the meeting encouraged freedom of expression and discussion of any issue by any member of the community. Patients expressed enjoyment over the fellowship and opportunity to see colleagues and friends from other units. They also enjoyed meeting patients newly admitted and being brought up to date on hospital news. Many patients also regarded the meeting as an entertaining or humorous diversion from their daily intensive therapy schedule. One patient summed up, "I enjoy hearing about other units, seeing new and familiar faces, hearing about current activities; I feel that I belong after each community meeting."

DISCUSSION

The question of validation of the proposition that the community meeting can be conducted as an effective large group psychotherapy remains unanswered. Methodological problems of evaluating psychotherapy are well known, particularly when the prescription, so to speak, is multifactorial, as is the case with the many components of treatment at Elmcrest. It is possible to assess the overall treatment program in terms of "before and after" clinical assessment of patients. Such studies simply measure treatment outcome in terms of the patient's follow-up clinical state after discharge. But to compartmentalize that result and to evaluate separately such components of treatment as chemotherapy, family therapy, community meetings, small group therapy, or individual therapy would be a formidable, if not impossible, task and this has not been addressed in this report. The rationale, then, of ascribing therapeutic value to any particular component of the treatment program rests on the context of that activity, its process and phenomenology, plus the patient's immediate responses to that component of therapy. Thus, if a patient is, for example, in art therapy, and during the time spent there becomes symptom-free, stimulated, socialized, communicative, experimental, and creative, we then would feel justified to judge that experience as a therapeutic one even though we might not know the duration, outcome, or generalizability of the patient's responses. That is to say, we would be willing to view patients' immediate responses to art therapy sessions as presumptive evidence that the experience of art therapy does qualify as a therapy.

This, then, is the rather thin rationale for stating that the large group community meeting does qualify as a group psychotherapy, that the behavioral responses of patients in the context of the meeting appear to be consistent with therapeutic experience. The community meetings seem consistently to produce spontaneous communicative interactions, intense emotionality, and unfreezing of stereotyped behavior with new adaptive behavior occurring on the part of participants. Descriptions of the community meetings also suggest a common ground with small group psychotherapy: chaotic beginnings with disjointed, unrelated expressions of affect-laden complaints are gradually replaced by struggles for focus, structure, and leadership. The struggle is accompanied by expressions of frustration, anger, and disappointment but, finally, there is gradual emergence of sustained, patterned sharing and supportive relevant responsiveness. This process also has been described by Rogers (1977). The large therapy group seems to move with much difficulty and tension toward building a supportive, nurturing therapeutic community. The meetings frequently end on a single focus, theme, or person as the group's agenda. This sequence characterizes many of our community meetings. They start as chaotic, followed by gradual pulling together around a theme or person, with a final ending on a high level of synchronized coordination among the various subgroups. A sense of togetherness, competence, strength, and excitement prevails in the group's mastery over chaos and negativity.

Staff contributions include role modeling and verbal sharing of inner responses and concerns. Simple descriptive observations of group behavior stated in a nonjudgmental way seem to contribute to the organizing process and to promote implicit and explicit attitudes of trust among patients and staff. The concern, respect, positive regard, and focus on process rather than on content or outcome characterize staff interventions. The willingness of staff to accept patients as a group of persons with common and shared concerns, needs, and aspirations is essential. The staff conveys trust that the group will find its own way, its own strength, its own purpose and leadership without staff imposing condescending leadership or structure upon them.

Large group experiences can be powerful, dramatic, and profound for all categories of participants, not only when the participants are competent credentialed professionals, as in a Tavistock conference, but even when the group consists of hospitalized, severely disordered mental patients, half of them adolescents. The normalizing, socializing, antipsychotic, antineurotic, antidependency effects of the experience qualify the large group community meeting as a potent form of group psychotherapy.

The large group not only can be an effective group psychotherapy, but also is an effective sociotherapy as defined by Edelson (1970). The large group meeting does promote resolution of inter- and intra-group tensions and conflicts. The subgroups of the hospital are in continuous interplay. Individuals become spokesmen in the community meeting for their subgroups, such as their ward or units, age group, diagnosis, or behavior pathology. The differences between large group and small group psychotherapy appear to be insignificant. There seems to be no compelling reasons why the rationale for small group psychotherapy should not also apply to large group psychotherapy.

A frequent criticism of the community meeting being conducted as a large group therapy is that it is too stressful, that it is not easily controllable by the therapists, and that there is too much risk of violence. However, one could make the case that all effective psychotherapies require the introduction of some stress in terms of the therapy threatening the patient's behavioral status quo. The therapist and the therapy are pitted against the defenses and neurotic behavior patterns of the patient. Thus, built into psychotherapy is always something like a struggle. The competence of therapists includes being able to titrate that stress and keep it at a constructive level rather than as a destructive, pathogenic, or catastrophic experience.

In a general sense the community meeting as therapy offers patients an opportunity for differentiation and autonomization. It may be a fearful experience to stand up and speak in the community meeting, but to do so does increase the patient's sense of autonomy and individuality. Patients can be observed becoming more and more differentiated and less and less fused with their group as their hospital experience evolves. In the preface to his book *The Large Group: Dynamics and Therapy*, Lionel Kreeger wrote that the whole field of psychotherapy was rapidly expanding and in the last decade interest had turned toward the large group. He maintained that as a result of the inclusion of large group experience both in therapeutic institutions and training schemes, the potential of large group therapy began to emerge. He observed that all those who have worked with large groups acknowledge the fascination and power that they hold and most would agree that they present a new dimension to our understanding of group dynamics. He concluded that the place of large group therapy was still to be defined (Kreeger 1975).

REFERENCES

Bion, W. R. (1959). *Experiences in Groups*. New York: Basic Books.

Burrow, T. (1927). The group method of analysis. *Psychoanalytic Review* 19:268–280.

Caudill, W. (1958). *The Psychiatric Hospital as a Small Society*. Cambridge: Harvard University Press.

Curry, A. E. (1967). Large therapeutic groups: a critique and appraisal of selected literature. *International Journal of Group Psychotherapy*, October, vol. 17, no. 4.

Edelson, M. (1970). *Sociotherapy and Psychotherapy*. Chicago: University of Chicago Press.

Ezriel, H. (1950). A psychoanalytic approach to group treatment. *British Journal of Medical Psychiatry* 23:59.

Fairweather, G. W. (1969). *Community Life for the Mentally Ill: An Alternative to Institutional Care*. Chicago: Aldine.

Foulkes, S. H. (1964). *Therapeutic Group Analysis*. London: Allen and Unwin.

Freud, S. (1921). Group psychology and the analysis of the ego. *Standard Edition* 18: 69–143.

Jones, M. (1953). *The Therapeutic Community*. New York: Basic Books.

Kreeger, L. (1975). *The Large Group: Dynamics and Therapy*. London: Constable.

Lewin, K. (1935). *A Dynamic Theory of Personality*. New York: McGraw-Hill.

Minear, J. (1979). Evaluation of the weekly community meeting. Personal communication.

Moreno, J. L. (1958). *The First Book of Group Psychotherapy*. New York: Beacon House.

Rapoport, R. (1960). *The Community as Doctor*. London: Tavistock.

Rice, A. K., and Turquet, P. M. (1965). *Learning for Leadership: Interpersonal and Intergroup Relations*. London: Tavistock.

Rioch, D. M. (1953). Milieu therapy. *Psychiatry* 16:65–72.

Rogers, C. R. (1977). Learnings in large groups: their implications for the future. La Jolla, CA: Center for Studies of the Person. Private publication.

Schilder, P. (1938): *Psychotherapy*. New York: Norton.

Slavson, S. R. (1947). *The Practice of Group Therapy*. New York: International Universities Press.

———(1956). *The Fields of Group Psychotherapy*. New York: International Universities Press.

Turquet, P. M. (1975). Threats to identity in the large group. In *The Large Group: Dynamics and Therapy*, ed. L. Kreeger. London: Constable.

Appendix 3

FAMILY THERAPY IN PSYCHIATRIC HOSPITAL TREATMENT[1]

Prior to 1960, treatment of the families of hospitalized psychiatric patients was mainly concerned with allaying guilt and other feelings associated with the mental illness of the identified patient. The psychiatric social worker within a hospital setting would obtain the clinical history from family members and also answer questions by the family regarding hospital routine. Family involvement in intake or subsequent treatment was usually peripheral and rarely routine. Even in child guidance clinics, families were rarely involved in the treatment process, but rather, using a team approach, the psychiatrist saw the child, the social worker dealt separately with the family, and the psychologist would administer psychological tests to the child. This compartmentalization of the family usually excluded the father entirely. When family therapy was used in hospital treatment, it was largely adjunctive, something secondary to the individual psychotherapy, group therapy, or biological or physical therapies being offered.

However, in the 1950s, work with schizophrenic patients by a number of clinicians led to new awareness of the importance of the family in terms of pathogenesis, pathology, and treatment. Murray Bowen (1957, 1961, 1965) called for involvement of families in the therapeutic process, and, coincidentally, Ackerman and Behrens (1956, 1958), Jackson (1958), Satir (1964), and Whitaker (1967) also wrote on this subject, laying the groundwork for a theory and practice of family therapy. Others, such as Bateson and colleagues (1956), Framo (1975), Haley (1963), Lidz (1968), Minuchin (1975), Watzlawick and colleagues (1957), and Wynne (1965) should be mentioned.

Family therapy practice also was influenced by the "human potential" and encounter group movements of the 1950s and 1960s. These developments led to the evolving of a here-and-now active interventionist approach in family therapy and contributed to the establishment of family therapy as a primary subspecialty in clinical psychiatry, psychology, and social work. J. L. Moreno's (1946) work in reconstructing family history in psychodrama contributed to the subsequent development of family therapy theory. The application of general systems theory to the field of human behavior by L. Von Bertalanffy (1966) also played a part in the evolution of family therapy.

However, in the course of its evolution as a major component of psychosocial treatment, family therapy theory and practice split into two alternative models, paralleling the conflicting models of individual and group psychotherapy, namely, between directive and nondirective approaches. Orientations that lent themselves to directive and strategic interventions in family therapy derived from the work of Minuchin, Haley, Bowen, Papp, and Watzlawick. They espoused strategic, directive, and active interventions for problem solving by family therapists. They also proposed strategic and directive interventions by the therapist to change basic family configurations. The school of family therapy that rejects and opposes strategic, directive interventionist approaches seems to have fewer proponents than the directive strategic mode. Virginia Satir and Carl Whitaker are well-known representatives of the nonstrategic approach. This group of therapists espouses a more existential, humanistic, nonauthoritarian stance, emphasizing and offering spontaneous interpersonal intimacy and communication by the therapist as the preferred approach for effective family therapy. Nonstrategic family therapists show relatively less concern than the directive schools for explicit or direct problem solving in treatment and view problem solving by the family as an outcome of therapy rather than as a focus or goal of therapy itself.

Christian Beels and Andrew Ferber (1969) have classified family therapists on the basis of what they call conductors or reactors. They also subdivide the reactor group into analysts and systems purists. We note that Beels and Ferber categorize Virginia Satir as a conductor.

A FAMILY-ORIENTED PSYCHIATRIC HOSPITAL

As newly appointed (1971) medical director of a private psychiatric hospital with fifty-two beds in 1971, expanded to 105 beds in 1974, the author decided to design and implement a family therapy program for all patients admitted to the hospital. The author was influenced not only by the family therapists cited above, but also by the concepts of nondirective psychotherapy developed by Hellmuth Kaiser (Fierman 1965). Kaiser was a training psychoanalyst who, late in his career, shifted from traditional psychoanalytic techniques to an existential, communicative nondirective stance in his therapy. Murray Bowen was influenced by Kaiser while both were teaching at the Menninger Foundation, and Bowen's theories on dedifferentiation of family members contain elements of Kaiser's fusion theories. A Kaiserian approach applied to family therapy defines the task of the family therapist simply as providing a communicative experience by the therapist for all the members of the family. The intent of the therapy is to move all family members in the direction of becoming "defused," that is, to facilitate the freeing of each family member from fusion relationships with one another by accepting themselves (or more precisely, to stop denying themselves) as differentiated, separate individuals in their family. Using this communicative approach, the family therapist invites all the members of the family to relate as therapists to one another, thereby making each family therapy session an experience in intimate interpersonal encountering.

FAMILY THERAPY AS GROUP THERAPY

Using Kaiser's orientation, the essence of intra-family pathology is conceptualized as being that family members relate to one another as though they were fused and interconnected, and as though the focus of power and decision making for each individual family member was somehow projected into members other than themselves. Family members do not function as separate and autonomous beings within their family.

The goal of this family therapy is the same as the goal of group psychotherapy, to promote psychological separateness, autonomy, maturity, and independence in its members. This is done in both family and group psychotherapy by freeing family or group members from their patterns of relating to other people in a fused way, which distorts the reality of their individuality and separateness. The presence of actual family members in family therapy facilitates the therapeutic process of group therapy. These concepts are similar to Bowen's theory of the undifferentiated family ego mass resulting from pathological triangular relationships leading to family behavior pathology. Thus, group therapy may be conceptualized as surrogate family therapy. Similarly, family therapy may be conceptualized as group therapy with actual family members present. This line of reasoning has led the author to use surrogate family therapy for hospitalized patients who, for one reason or another, have no family members to participate in family therapy. Volunteer staff members, uninvolved in the patient's treatment, serve as surrogate family members in ongoing family therapy.

FAMILY THERAPY FOR DISCHARGE PLANNING

Family therapy in hospital settings is relevant to both of the two principal functions of hospitalization, that is, to provide effective psychosocial therapy and to provide competent administrative management of the patient. It is important that the management of the patient be differentiated conceptually and instrumentally from his psychotherapy. Management of the hospitalized patient is, of necessity, goal-directed, symptom-oriented, and concerned with discharge planning and the return and rehabilitation of the patient to his home and community. These goals of patient management should be differentiated from the goal of psychotherapy, which is to promote psychological autonomy, independence, and freedom from neurotic response patterns. Psychotherapy is cure-oriented and extends far beyond the period of hospitalization. The work of patient management and patient psychotherapy is ideally done by separate staff members. The patient's administrative therapist ideally should not be the patient's psychotherapist. There are considerable advantages in conceptualizing the two approaches and goals differently and separately, and also negative consequences in failing to do so. Power struggles, resistance to therapy, acting out, and noncompliance are facilitated by having the same individuals function as both administrative therapists and psychosocial therapists. Family therapy, however, is relevant to both administrative and psychotherapeutic goals. Family therapy can provide not only a potent and effective psychotherapy, but also a format for effective patient management and discharge planning. Issues concerning discharge depend heavily on the state of affairs within the patient's family. Discharge planning is best begun at the time of admission, and the patient's family should be invited to participate.

DISADVANTAGES OF INPATIENT FAMILY THERAPY

One major disadvantage of family therapy in hospitals is, of course, that the patient and the family must meet the heavy financial burden of hospitalization in addition to the costs of therapy. Another major disadvantage is that the hospitalized family member can hardly avoid being identified by others in the family as the "sick" member, thereby facilitating the resistance of other family members to deny their own psychological disorder or need for change or therapy.

Ideal family therapy sees all members of the family as separate, albeit interdependent, individuals in a family social system that has failed to permit all its members to experience optimum mental health and to reach full human potential. The hospitalized patient has been separated physically from his family, community, and job, and although this may be unavoidable because of the severity of the patient's disability, it creates problems in its own right and tends to foster dependency on the institution. In addition, the unavoidable turnover of patients, groups, and staff therapists in the hospital introduces instability into the family therapy experience.

ADVANTAGES OF INPATIENT FAMILY THERAPY

The advantages of family therapy for inpatients are significant. The authority of the hospital plus the crisis situation of the patient greatly facilitate involving the family and significant others in the patient's treatment. Hospital therapists can schedule intensive, high-frequency psychotherapy with sessions several times a week or even daily. Family therapy within the hospital is done in a controlled environment. In a hospital therapeutic community, the patient's patterns of relating to others can be more easily related to his family therapy.

Multiple family therapy is a valuable supplement to individual family therapy and is easily arranged during hospitalization (Haley et al. 1974). The patient and his family meet at least weekly with other patients and their families in a large group therapy. The families relate to one another in ways usually found to be supportive, informative, and therapeutic.

RATIONALE FOR FAMILY THERAPY ORIENTED HOSPITALIZATION

The rationale for prescribing family therapy for all hospitalized psychiatric patients is the theory that all psychopathology and behavior pathology is derived either entirely or in part from one's family of origin, and reinforced and exacerbated in the context of one's family of procreation. The issues of growth and development in family life are so central and crucial to the development of psychological health or disorder that the decision to prescribe family therapy as a basic part of treatment for all hospitalized psychiatric patients seems compelling, and has been confirmed clinically.

A hospital treatment program including intensive family therapy for all inpatients is possible for reasonably low cost. Families should be urged at the time of the patient's admission to come to the hospital for therapy at least three times a week, including multiple family therapy once a week.

SURROGATE FAMILY THERAPY

To patients for whom all significant family members are absent, deceased, uncooperative, or too distant, the hospital offers surrogate family therapy. The patient selects hospital staff and other patients who agree to participate as surrogate family members. The result is a combination of psychodrama and family therapy. This experiment has had favorable results and is now done routinely at the hospital. On one occasion a patient was admitted into the hospital by court order because of delinquency and violent behavior. He reported that he had no family relatives who were willing to have any connections with him, but that he was a member of a Hell's Angels motorcycle gang. The staff invited his Hell's Angels group to come to the hospital to serve as his surrogate family in family therapy. Each day these youths would roar up to the hospital en masse on their motorcycles garbed in their black leather jackets and proceed to function effectively as his family in therapy.

SIMULTANEOUS ADMISSION OF MULTIPLE FAMILY MEMBERS

Another innovation in the use of family therapy in this hospital has been the practice of admitting two or more members of a family simultaneously or during overlapping periods. Over the past 8 years approximately forty-five multiple family members were admitted. Of the forty-five, only about five family units were admitted simultaneously, that is, two or more members of the family admitted on the same day. The other instances were when additional family members were admitted days after the initial family member was admitted. This usually was a result of the impact of family therapy itself on the other family members. That is, the initial patient would be admitted to the hospital, and as family therapy evolved it became clear that the identified patient was not the only or even the most disturbed or disordered or needy person in the family, and so a second and, on some occasions, a third member of the family subsequently would be admitted. A modus operandi was established in the hospital to try, whenever possible, to assign the members of the family to different wards or units in the hospital. The individual family members thus would live in different units, but their family therapy arrangements were combined by negotiations between the staffs of the different units. The rationale is to provide the structure for separation for each family member, and to prevent coercion and intimidation between the various family members. Each family member has a base for separate living plus opportunity for as much family interaction and family therapy as seems helpful.

Family members were admitted simultaneously when they were referred for hospitalization as a family unit. In each of these instances they were pairs: husband and wife, two sisters, mother and daughter, and two brothers. In other instances family admissions occurred as fallout from family therapy. The combinations of subsequent admissions included husband and wife, father and son, father and daughter, mother and son, mother and daughter, and brother and sister.

Case History

A 37-year-old woman was admitted because of expressed suicidal preoccupation. Her husband had left her five years previously, and she had become increasingly alcoholic and depressed. Her husband had remarried but maintained intermittent contact with his two daughters, aged 20 and 15. The mother was in individual therapy for a year, but her course deteriorated and she was finally hospitalized. The older daughter dropped out of college. Depressed over her parents' divorce, she had trouble adjusting at college and felt rejected by her peers. During family therapy she confessed suicidal preoccupation and was admitted within a week after her mother. The 15-year-old younger daughter became agitated and, during sessions of family therapy, admitted to being heavily involved in drug abuse and was conflicted over peer pressures. She was admitted three weeks after her sister, one month after her mother. Each family member was housed in a separate hospital unit: the youngest on an adolescent unit, the 20-year-old on an adult unit, and the mother in another adult unit. They were prescribed daily family therapy sessions together, as well as group therapy separately. They all participated in the hospital-wide therapeutic community programs. The divorced father was persuaded to join the family therapy along with his new wife. There were heavy emotional confrontations and expressions and externalization of many suppressed feelings of resentment toward one another, and toward the parents and their divorce. As family therapy progressed, there was gradual reconciliation between family members and, approximately two months later, the mother left the hospital to continue treatment with her outside therapist. Family therapy continued for the daughters after the mother left the hospital. One week later the older daughter left to return to college and continued individual therapy there. One month later the younger daughter, who had been attending the hospital school, left the hospital. Since then, all have continued with family therapy in their home town.

In some instances involving married couples admitted simultaneously, the couple was assigned initially to separate units. Later on, after therapies were successful in bringing about change in their relationship, the couple then was moved into the same hospital unit and provided with a private room to share. This practice prevents the couple from being forced to be together prematurely at the outset of their hospital experience.

FAMILY THERAPY FOR PATIENTS WITH ACUTE PSYCHOTIC BEHAVIOR

Another innovative or experimental use of family therapy in the hospital is in the admitting unit when a violent, agitated, disorganized, disoriented, acutely psychotic patient is brought in. Rather than chemical restraints, physical restraints are preferred to immobilize the patient, leaving him available for intensive psychosocial therapy including family therapy. Psychotic behavior is viewed as purposeful communication rather than as irrational behavior. Chemotherapy for behavioral control is used as a last resort, only after psychosocial intervention is tried first, and an intensive marathon family therapy in the admitting unit is attempted. In a fair number of trials the patient has been "talked down," and violence decompressed after hours of therapy time by staff and family. Psychotic patients have been returned to a more rational and communicative state of mind within a few days of intensive psychosocial intervention including marathon family therapy sessions.

MOTIVATING FAMILIES FOR INPATIENT FAMILY THERAPY

At the time of admission there is usually a great deal of emotional investment by the family to have their relative admitted for treatment. This is a strategic time to motivate families to commit themselves to family therapy. The family is told at that time that they are expected to participate fully in the treatment program. Arrangements for time and frequency of sessions are made. If the family has not accompanied the patient during admission, they are phoned and told that their relative has been hospitalized and that their participation in therapy is required. The tension and sense of crisis during the admission process is used as effective leverage for family involvement. Studies have shown that there is little correlation between need for hospitalization and diagnosis, severity of illness, or degree of disability. But one consistent factor in hospitalization is the attitude of the family toward the patient in regard to hospitalization itself. The family's desire to extrude this member plus the member's wish to leave the family determines his hospitalization. Conversely, the family's desire to receive him back home plus the patient's wish to leave determines his discharge. Obviously, other factors are involved as well, such as diagnosis and degree of disability. But if the family is willing to accommodate itself to even horrendous and difficult behavior by a family member at home, they can and will do so. A significant part of the admission process involves motivating the family for family therapy. Family therapy is often scheduled for evenings or late afternoons to accommodate working family members.

Noncompliance by family members is remarkably rare

but may occur initially or a few days or weeks after family therapy has begun. However, much pressure can be brought to bear to prevent this. Strategic pressure is placed upon the patient, who is held responsible for family noncompliance. Frequently it is the patient himself who is overtly or covertly discouraging family members from coming. It is assumed that if the patient really wants the family there, he is able to see that they attend. Frequently, family members will drop out because they find the experience too threatening or traumatic, rather than because of lack of interest in the patient. The therapist must deal with these issues by anticipating, recognizing, and confronting noncompliance and by helping the family externalize and verbalize their concerns.

TRAINING STAFF FOR FAMILY THERAPY

Nursing personnel including mental health workers are assigned to a program of training in family therapy. A full year of training is required before one can actually function as a primary family therapist, but during that year each trainee participates as co-therapist with a senior therapist, and receives didactic, videotape, and workshop training. Psychologists, social workers, and psychiatrists also provide family therapy and also function as consultants, teachers, supervisors, and co-therapists for nursing personnel.

A prime task of senior clinical staff is that of the supervision and training of the family therapists. This has led to some difficulties. The number of trained and skilled family therapists is small, and to locate family therapists who can also teach has been an important consideration in the hospital's hiring practices. A number of difficulties occur in the training program. Nurses and mental health workers can be hesitant about taking on the roles of therapists, but once they overcome their initial fears they tend to swing to the other pole and behave as if anything and everything they do could be called therapy. This requires continuous supervision and training of such personnel. It also necessitates an ongoing training program for the senior clinicians so that they can continue to acquire the skills required to deal with their trainees.

CONCLUSION

The primary task of inpatient family therapy is to provide psychotherapeutic experiences for the hospitalized patient. Patients enter the hospital in crisis. The goal of hospital treatment and management is to effect the earliest possible return to the community and to motivate the patient to continue treatment after discharge to prevent relapse and readmission. Prerequisite for discharge is a firm discharge plan that includes identification and actual contact with a follow-up individual and/or family therapist who sees the patient several times prior to discharge from the hospital. There should be overlapping of inpatient and outpatient therapy experiences. Issues concerning discharge become the initial focus of family therapy. However, as therapy evolves, the focus shifts to core conflicts within the family as well as rehabilitation, vocational, and adjustment issues of the patient. Inpatient family therapy provides a crucial and potent contribution to both effective psychiatric hospital treatment and effective discharge planning. These are the two essentials of successful hospital treatment.

REFERENCES

Ackerman, N. W., and Behrens, M. L. (1956). A study of family diagnosis. *American Journal of Orthopsychiatry* 23:26–78.

———(1958). *The Psychodynamics of Family Life*. New York: Basic Books.

Bateson, F., Jackson, D., Haley, J., and Weakland, J. (1956). Toward a theory of schizophrenia. *Behavior Science* 1:251–264.

Beels, C., and Ferber, A. (1969). Family therapy: a view. *Family Process* 8:280–318.

Bowen, M. (1957). *Family participation in schizophrenia*. Paper presented at the annual meeting of the American Psychiatric Association, Chicago, May.

———(1961). Family psychotherapy. *American Journal of Orthopsychiatry* 31:40–60.

———(1965). Family psychotherapy with schizophrenia in the hospital and in private practice. In *Intensive Family Therapy*, ed. H. Boszormenyi-Nagy and J. Framo, pp. 213–243. New York: Harper and Row.

Fierman, L., ed. (1965). *Effective Psychotherapy—The Contribution of Hellmuth Kaiser*. New York: Free Press.

Framo, J. L. (1975). Personal reflections of a family therapist. *Journal of Marriage and Family Counseling* 1:15–28.

Haley, J. (1963). *Strategies of Psychotherapy*. New York: Grune & Stratton.

Haley, J., Alqueurp, B., Labuit, H. A., and Moronge, D. (1974). Multiple family therapy—further developments in changing families. In *A Family Therapy Reader*, pp. 82–95. New York: Grune & Stratton.

Jackson, D. (1958). *Family interaction, family homeosta-*

sis and some implications for conjoint family psychotherapy. Paper presented at the meeting of the Academy of Psychoanalysis, New York, May.

Lidz, T. (1968). *The Person*. New York: Basic Books.

Minuchin, S. (1975). *Families and Family Therapy*. Cambridge: Harvard University Press.

Moreno, J. L. (1946). *Psychodrama*. New York: Beacon House.

Satir, V. (1964). *Conjoint Family Therapy*. Palo Alto: Science and Behavior Books.

Von Bertalanffy, L. (1966). General system theory and psychiatry. In *American Handbook of Psychiatry*, vol. 3, ed. S. Arieti, pp. 705–721. New York: Basic Books.

Watzlawick, P., Beaver, J. H., and Jackson, D. D. (1957). *Pragmatics of Human Communication*. New York: Norton.

Whitaker, C. A. (1967). The growing edge in techniques of family therapy. In *Techniques of Family Therapy*, ed. J. Haley and L. Hoffman. New York: Basic Books.

Wynne, L. (1965). Some indications and contraindications for exploring family therapy. In *Intensive Family Therapy*, ed. H. Boszormenyi-Nagy and J. Framo. New York: Harper and Row.

Appendix 4

EMERGENCY: SEVEN DIALOGUES REFLECTING THE ESSENCE OF PSYCHOTHERAPY IN AN EXTREME ADVENTURE[1]

Hellmuth Kaiser

PROLOGUE

Just as the normal function of an organ or an organism is frequently illuminated by pathologic events, so the views of a therapist on the essential nature of his daily work may become unusually lucid when they are applied to an extreme and unusual case, which is theoretically possible but has never occurred in real life.

The following seven dialogues sketch such an unusual case. The views of the therapist in the story are my views. They are not easy to present or to transmit, not because they imply a complicated theory, but because they are simple where one expects the elaborate. When they are expressed in abstract terms, as a textbook would do, the reader is likely to miss their meaning, as if he had to decipher a melody from the grooves of a gramophone disk.

The sequence of scenes contains, in condensation, interaction between the therapist and his patient. However, I do not intend to prove, but only to show.

SCENE 1

Dr. Terwin's office. Dr. Terwin is in the process of clearing his desk, as he usually does before leaving for the day. He picks up a letter and gets caught up in reading it through.

Secretary: Dr. Terwin—Dr. Terwin!

Dr. Terwin [his eyes still on the letter]: Yes, Linda?

Secretary: You didn't forget that you still have to see a patient?

Dr. Terwin: A patient?

Secretary: You know—the lady who phoned this afternoon, Mrs. Estella Porfiri.

Dr. Terwin [hardly remembering]: Oh yes, something urgent, didn't you say?

Secretary: Right, Doctor, she made it sound very urgent indeed!

Dr. Terwin [good-naturedly]: You never know; it might be a real emergency.

Secretary: Anyway, she seemed dead set on seeing you today, no matter what. But I can tell you now: When she complains about lack of will power, general apathy, and no interest in life—don't believe a word of it!

Dr. Terwin: Who knows?

Secretary: I know! May I leave? Or. . . .

Dr. Terwin: By all means! Enjoy yourself!

Secretary: Thank you. Good-bye, Dr. Terwin!

Dr. Terwin [after another look at the letter]: O.K. *[He opens the door to the waiting room.]* Mrs. Porfiri, I assume?

Mrs. Porfiri [entering]: How do you do, Dr. Terwin!

Dr. Terwin: How do you do! Will you sit down here, Mrs. Porfiri?

Mrs. Porfiri sits down and looks attentively at Dr. Terwin, who takes a chair facing her. She seems surprised by his appearance.

Mrs. Porfiri: You look so different from what I had expected!

Dr. Terwin [with a little smile]: Maybe you came to the wrong person. I am *Simon F.* Terwin.

Mrs. Porfiri: No, no! Dr. Simon F. Terwin. There is no other Dr. Terwin in the whole city. You know Dr. Redstone, do you?

Dr. Terwin: Dr. Oliver Redstone? He was one of my teachers.

Mrs. Porfiri: I know! *[She lapses into a thoughtful silence.]*

Dr. Terwin: I understood you were in a kind of emergency?

Mrs. Porfiri: Because I insisted on seeing you as soon as possible? I have been in fear for a long time—especially in the last four months. And I did not know what to do. And then suddenly, I learned that you were in the city—that you have been in this very city for something like a quarter of a year. *[With a faint smile]* So I felt I should not lose any more time!

Dr. Terwin: I am not sure that I understand you fully.

Do you mean to say that Dr. Redstone referred you to me?

Mrs. Porfiri: He did, but I should rather say he confirmed my opinion. I'll explain in a minute! *[Tensely]* May I ask you a question first?

[Dr. Terwin looks somewhat astonished and waits.]

Mrs. Porfiri: It is very important to me. All depends . . .

Dr. Terwin: Of course! What do you want to know?

Mrs. Porfiri: About half a year ago I read an article of yours—I forget the title—was it "Talking to People" in the *Clinical Psychologist*?

Dr. Terwin: That's right.

Mrs. Porfiri [quickly]: There you said something like, "In order to treat a person, nothing more is required than that the therapist meets this person regularly for a sufficient time in his office. There are no rules for the patient. He need not talk about any specific topics or talk at all." I want to know whether you mean this literally. *[She looks at Dr. Terwin in great suspense.]*

Dr. Terwin [smiling]: The answer is yes.

Mrs. Porfiri [repeating his word]: Yes. Good—that's very important. *[She seems to rest from the effort of settling this question and to ponder about the next step.]* You—you don't think that it matters where the doctor sees the patient?

Dr. Terwin: I don't know what you have in mind. I would not want to see a patient in—let's say, a restaurant.

Mrs. Porfiri: Of course, of course! That's not what I meant. There is really no point in trying . . .

Dr. Terwin: Trying what?

Mrs. Porfiri [impatiently]: Oh, my God, to trap you! Can't you see? To get you to commit yourself by answering my general questions, so that you cannot back out when I beg your help in my special case! But it won't work! If you are a coward, you will back out anyway!

Dr. Terwin: That might be. But I can neither back out nor accede to your request as long as I am completely in the dark as to what it is you are asking for.

Mrs. Porfiri [proudly]: I am not going to ask for a favor. I'll tell you what my fears are and you will either help or refuse to do so! You know who I am?

Dr. Terwin: I understood, Mrs. Estella Porfiri!

Mrs. Porfiri [waving her hand impatiently]: I mean, do you know my husband?

Dr. Terwin: You expect me to know him? Don't forget that it's been only three months since I moved to this city!

Mrs. Porfiri: Good, very good! I thought you might have heard the name: Dr. Emilio Porfiri, psychiatrist.

Dr. Terwin: I am sorry. The name sounds only vaguely familiar to me. I would not have known that he is a psychiatrist and lives in this city, if you had not said so.

Mrs. Porfiri: He is not very well known. He is 36, in private practice, and he hasn't published anything—oh, in the last five or six years. We have been married almost eight years. It may sound strange to you when I say that it has only been during the last two or, perhaps, three years that I have come to understand how unhappy Emilio really is. Or maybe it is not my better understanding—it might also be that in the beginning of our marriage he was not so unhappy or disturbed as he became later. I know that during the last four months a change for the worse has taken place.

Dr. Terwin: You would say that your husband is severely depressed?

Mrs. Porfiri: Oh, God, yes! Severely depressed! I don't mean that he goes around groaning and moaning; but there is no sparkle in his eye any more. He doesn't complain—or only very rarely. Seeing him from afar you wouldn't notice much. He is well controlled, has always been. He goes to his office, sees his patients, goes to meetings, and even gives speeches occasionally. But it is as if he were far away in his mind, only going through the motions of life.

Dr. Terwin: And you say all this has become more pronounced in the last—I think, four months you said?

Mrs. Porfiri: Yes—as far as I can tell; it began gradually, yet . . .

Dr. Terwin: Yet?

Mrs. Porfiri: I wanted to say that in the last four months he has become very restless, which he had not been before at all. You know, he used to design furniture; he was quite good at it. When we needed something he did the design. He liked to work it out carefully, and it always took him a long time to do it exactly the way he wanted to. Yet he always finished what he had started. Now he seems unable to stick with anything which is not absolutely necessary.

Dr. Terwin: When you say that there was a deterioration in the last four months, are you only making an estimate of the time, or can you think of an event which occurred four months ago?

Mrs. Porfiri: The latter, Dr. Terwin. There was an event which caused Emilio great concern and distress. And I don't doubt that it contributed in some way to the deterioration. Only, as you will see, it cannot be the clue to everything!

Dr. Terwin: You seem hesitant to describe this event.

Mrs. Porfiri [thoughtfully]: I am hesitant. It's silly, I know! I feel that this incident will bias you against Emilio, but, as you will see, there was really nothing he could have done to prevent it. It was simply hard luck. This is what happened: Emilio had a patient, a Mr. Dorand, whom he had seen for approximately two years. An addict! Four months ago, the patient, who had improved and seemed decidedly on the way up, had to interrupt treatment for two weeks. Some family problem. When he came back, a few days later than anticipated, he called my husband, as we learned from the answering service which had picked up the call. We got the message late on a Sunday afternoon. My husband called the patient's number several times, but there was no answer. He tried again in the evening; again no answer. The same happened Monday morning. But as soon as Emilio had left for the office, Mr. Dorand called. I told him that Dr. Porfiri had tried to reach him, and that Mr. Dorand should call him at his office in fifteen minutes. The patient remained silent a few seconds, but I could hear him clear his throat. Then the line went dead. I called his apartment, but there was no answer. Apparently he had called from somewhere else, and he never got back home. Somebody found his dead body Monday night in a little motel. Suicide! I have told all the details to show that, as far as I can see, Emilio had done all that could be done under the circumstances. It seemed natural that Emilio was terribly upset when he learned about the suicide. He canceled some of his hours; he went to the police, to the coroner, and to the morgue. He got in touch with the relatives. And for a week or so this unhappy event kept him occupied. I have asked myself, of course, and have asked Emilio more than once, whether his worrying on Sunday evening was completely accidental or whether he had any reason to suspect that something had gone wrong with the patient. "No reason," he said, "not the slightest bit of a reason. But, look, in spite of the lack of any reason I *was* worried, and you know I was. I must have made a mistake and must have known it without knowing when or how."

Dr. Terwin: What followed?

Mrs. Porfiri: Well, to the best of my recollection, Emilio recovered from the shock, I would say, within a week or two. But then—I cannot tell how it started. There must have been a slow transition or—well, I don't know. But he must have slid into his present behavior, this—what should I call it: aloofness, restlessness, silent despair—oh, it is uncanny!

Dr. Terwin: It frightens you?

Mrs. Porfiri: It does! Oh my God, it does!

Dr. Terwin: I understand your husband is working as before the—the accident?

Mrs. Porfiri: I think so. He keeps his hours, sees his patients. However, during these four months or so he has lost some other patients—not in the same way, of course, but two or three quit prematurely, as I understood. Emilio has mentioned that occasionally, but not as he would have done before—in former times, I mean. It used to concern him a good deal if a patient left without too good a reason, but now he doesn't seem to care. No, that's not right! He does care, but something has changed in him. I think sometimes that he takes the other side, Mr. Dorand's side—he used this expression once, in a different context, but it sticks in my mind.

Dr. Terwin: I see . . .

Mrs. Porfiri: Dr. Terwin, can you say anything? Can you help?

Dr. Terwin: Possibly! I would certainly be glad to talk to your husband. Isn't that what you have in mind?

Mrs. Porfiri [after sighing and then remaining silent for a few seconds]: I had it in mind. Of course, I had it in mind. I had it in mind a year ago, and during these last four months I've had little else in my mind. But, you know, he does not want to. Calmly and firmly, he refuses to see anybody.

Dr. Terwin: His reasons?

Mrs. Porfiri: I'm not sure that I can answer this question. He says it won't help him—something like that—but this can't be the real reason. How could he know without trying? I have asked, begged, implored him to try. But he seems unassailable.

Dr. Terwin: You know, your husband might simply need more time to make his decision. A psychiatrist has, perhaps, more serious obstacles to overcome than many who are not of the faculty.

Mrs. Porfiri [intently]: You tell me to wait?

Dr. Terwin: Let me ask: What is it you are so afraid of?

Mrs. Porfiri [in a low voice]: Suicide!

Dr. Terwin: I assume your husband moves in a circle of psychiatrists. It would be strange if not one of his friends has noticed the change in him which you have observed?

Mrs. Porfiri: I can't tell whether anybody has noticed. Nobody has said anything to me about it—with the exception of our maid. She asked me, oh, some weeks ago: "Is Dr. Porfiri ill? He doesn't seem to feel well." Dr. Terwin—believe me—oh, *do* believe me, it *is* urgent!

Dr. Terwin: Mrs. Porfiri, you will understand that I am in no position to confirm or deny the urgency of the case. *[As he notices a look of despair on her face, he goes on.]* Do not misunderstand me! I am ready to act on the assumption that there might be urgency. But I have to get some idea that my action would at least not make things worse! I refuse to act simply for the sake of giving you, or myself, the feeling that action has been taken! Let me ask: What do you think would happen if you told your husband that you had asked me to come and see him? Presenting him with a *fait accompli,* as it were? *[As she makes a gesture to interrupt and even starts to say something, he raises his hands to make her listen.]* Please, don't feel you have to decide in a hurry. Such a *fait accompli* method has an advantage and also a disadvantage, and which prevails depends essentially on the patient's personality. I want you to consider as calmly as you can these two sides. Look, when you want psychiatric help for your husband, you imply that his refusal to go to see somebody is unreasonable and its motivation irrational. You follow me?

Mrs. Porfiri: Yes, but. . . .

Dr. Terwin: All right, listen: We may then assume that what prevents him from consulting a colleague is something like shame or pride. More generally, he might consider it as wrong in some sense or other for him to admit to a colleague his worry, depression, or whatever it is. This would not exclude the possibility that he would like to have somebody help him, but his counter-motivation overrides the desire. If this were so, it might help to present him with a *fait accompli*. He would not feel so keenly that he himself is asking for help, because you had taken all the initiative. He might tell himself that not to talk to me, when I had been summoned by you, would be rude. So it would not be his doing if he talked to me, but rather yours.

Mrs. Porfiri: But, Dr. Terwin. . . .

Dr. Terwin: Allow me a minute more—we are not *that* much in a hurry. I said that there is a disadvantage, too, in the *fait accompli* method. I take it that he has no close friends. You are probably the only person at the present moment he feels close to and has some confidence in. Your calling in a psychiatrist, behind his back, as it were, your putting before him a *fait accompli* and trying to force him into treatment, might impress him most of all not as a sign of your caring for him and loving him, but as a sign that you have lost confidence in him—that you, well, declare him incompetent to look out for himself and are now acting like a guardian who forces onto his helpless ward what he, the guardian, thinks is best.

Mrs. Porfiri: That is exactly what I am afraid will happen! That's what I wanted to say all the time. Emilio is terribly sensitive about what he calls "people with the best intentions." He would cancel the appointment or, if it were too late for that, he might even leave the house. No, that *fait accompli* method has no chance and would be very, very dangerous.

Dr. Terwin: Hm! Your estimate as to your husband's reaction might be completely correct. But I am baffled! I thought you would take the opposite view. What, then, is it that you suggest? I understood you wanted to make a suggestion didn't you?

Mrs. Porfiri: I do want to make a suggestion. It is not by chance that I came to see you and no other psychiatrist. *[There is a short pause. She is highly conscious that this is the moment of decision.]* I called you the minute I learned you were here—or rather, I wired Dr. Redstone and called you as soon as I had heard from him. I have a very definite idea how you could help. You remember my question—the one I asked right at the beginning? Well, the answer you gave me confirmed what I had thought. Listen, Dr. Terwin, I can see that you can't simply take my word that there is danger. But, as you admitted—and I appreciate very much that you did—you also can't say for sure that I am in error. I know that I am going to ask something unusual from you—something, let's say, that is not usually done by a professional man. But, please, listen to me with an open mind! *[A little pause]* Let me say something more: Dr. Oliver Redstone is a friend of mine. I had talked with him earlier, over the phone. We had a long discussion. He is very old, but his mind is as sharp as ever. Well, his verdict was: "Not impossible! But who would dare to do it, and be able to do it?" Your name was mentioned. But you lived far away then. Now you will understand how I felt when I heard that you were here in this very city of ours—just now, when I need help more than ever. *[She pauses to catch her breath.]*

Dr. Terwin [in a low, almost dreamy voice]: Oliver Redstone! How strange! *[Without raising his voice, but very firmly]* And your suggestion, Mrs. Porfiri?

Mrs. Porfiri: It can't matter where you see your patient. Emilio is a therapist. So you could go and see him as his patient! *[Her voice is faltering.]*

Dr. Terwin: See him as his patient, you say?

Mrs. Porfiri [bravely]: As his patient. You would call him and make an appointment. He has sufficient time open. You wouldn't have to use another name. I know that psychiatrists occasionally ask colleagues for their professional help. *[She smiles breathlessly.]*

Dr. Terwin [in a controlled voice]: But he would ask how I came to consult him, wouldn't he?

Mrs. Porfiri: I thought of that. You could mention Dr. Redstone. He doesn't know Emilio personally very well, but he thinks well of him as a psychiatrist. And anyway he would agree to your using his name. He says so in his letter!

Dr. Terwin: As you have read my article so carefully and talked to my teacher and friend, Dr. Redstone, about me, you certainly must know that it is my conviction that treatment can't accomplish anything substantial as long as the therapist keeps pretending, lying, play-acting.

Mrs. Porfiri: I thought of that! Your objections against lying and pretending in such a case are not based, I understand, on moral principles. Are they?

Dr. Terwin: Correct! They are not!

Mrs. Porfiri: But on the thought that lying and cheating would interfere with treatment?

Dr. Terwin: Indeed, they would.

Mrs. Porfiri: Now, listen, Dr. Terwin, I thought of that too. It is true you will have to tell lies in the initial interview—you will have to say or indicate that you want treatment, and probably also why you want treatment. You will have to pretend, invent, lie, and cheat. But as soon as treatment starts, once you are accepted as a patient, you have the inalienable privilege of the patient to say what you like. And it is up to you to limit yourself to truthful statements and leave unsaid the essentially conventional formalities as to whom you consider to be the patient and whom you consider to be the therapist. *[She looks at him with the courage of desperation.]*

Dr. Terwin: Mrs. Porfiri, you suggest that I, a psychiatrist, call a colleague of mine, another psychiatrist, and ask him for his professional help, ask him to take me into treatment for some real or invented troubles of mine, while, in reality, I am hired by his wife to treat him. Do you realize what that means?

Mrs. Porfiri [proudly]: I know what it means! It means doing the only thing which could probably save him!

Dr. Terwin [with a faint smile]: That is your point of view, which I certainly respect. But it is not the only possible one. I listened to you, as you asked me to, with a fairly open mind. Now I would like you to return the favor! *[He looks her straight in the face; she answers in the affirmative with a minimal nod.]*

Dr. Terwin: If everything goes well and we get over the point *[he wants to say,* "which I shudder to think of," *but suppresses this remark and replaces it by taking a deep breath]* when I can tell your husband what it's all about, and we can continue the treatment in a more—usual way—it won't matter so much if the thing becomes known—it can be played down. My colleagues will call me a screwball, no doubt, but nothing succeeds like success. As long as neither you nor Dr. Porfiri complains, nothing much can happen. But it would be childish—or worse, it would be ludicrous, megalomanic, idiotic, irresponsible—not to consider the possibility of failure. Let's say that after three months or so I come to the conviction that I am getting nowhere. Please realize that something like that may happen under absolutely normal conditions of treatment, while here the conditions would be extremely unfavorable. In a normal case, I would not worry. I know that it frequently takes more time to tune in, to hear the patient accurately, to acquire the necessary precision of perception. Yet in this case, which would be as new to me as doing psychotherapy with the pet wife of an Arabian sheik whose prisoner I was, I wouldn't know where to look for a helpful idea. I would never know whether it was only I who was not perceptive enough, or whether it was the damned situation I was in which limited my means of expression. If I got desperate enough, I would back out. It wouldn't be too hard to make my withdrawal plausible—at least as plausible as the quitting of most patients who stop prematurely, where nobody can ever tell for sure just what made them quit. But worse might happen. We cannot exclude the possibility that Dr. Porfiri might become suspicious. And then what?

Mrs. Porfiri: Oh God! You are right. We cannot exclude every danger. But you can be sure that as long as *you* didn't confess about our agreement, and I didn't, Emilio would always respect you as a patient and would rather accuse himself of a paranoid delusion and break off the treatment than accuse you of—of—being an imposter. I can assure you of one thing: Come hell or high water, neither I nor Dr. Redstone will admit as much as even the thought of our agreement, whoever might ask us about it.

Dr. Terwin [murmuring]: Crazy, crazy! So what if—your suggestion. . . .

Mrs. Porfiri: Dr. Terwin, let me ask this: When you, for a moment, disregard the unusualness of my suggestion and the trouble it might cause you with your colleagues or your conscience, do you think it could have a chance of success?

Dr. Terwin [looking at her thoughtfully]: A chance of success? Heavens, what do you think I am arguing about? The answer is: Yes, a chance! *[For a whole minute the two stare at each other, sometimes frowning, sometimes smiling, obviously intent on reading the other's mind.]*

Mrs. Porfiri [starts crying. After 20 seconds she manages

to say between sobs]: Excuse me, Dr. Terwin! I have no words any more.

Dr. Terwin [confused and embarrassed]: But—but—I—I did not say anything yet! You, you—don't—have to feel so—desperate.

Mrs. Porfiri [with a faint smile through her tears]: I don't cry out of despair. I—I am so—grateful!

Dr. Terwin: Who of us is the therapist? How could you know? Anyway, you are right. So cry if you feel like it!

Mrs. Porfiri [somewhat recovered]: I—I have this letter from Dr. Redstone—it might help some.

Dr. Terwin [taking the letter without looking at it]: Is there anybody besides Dr. Redstone to whom you have talked about your plan?

Mrs. Porfiri: Nobody!

Dr. Terwin: Good! Don't talk to anybody, no matter what happens. And don't get in touch with me as long as the experiment lasts. No need to complicate matters. Should I find it necessary to back out, I'll let you know. Do you think you can agree to that?

Mrs. Porfiri: I agree. About the fee—will you read the letter first?

Dr. Terwin [reads mumbling to himself for a while, then aloud]: "I declare that if Dr. Terwin should decide to undertake it, he has my full approval. I ask him in this case to send his statements for the time he will spend and the money he pays as fee to Dr. Porfiri to me. I'll take full financial responsibility for the whole treatment." So that takes care of that. Do you have any more questions?

Mrs. Porfiri: No, I can't think of any. You know how grateful I am!

Dr. Terwin: That's all right. Let's see what happens. I'll call your husband tomorrow. *[Both get up.]* Good luck, Mrs. Porfiri!

Mrs. Porfiri: I feel hopeful!

SCENE 2

Dr. Terwin's office. He is dictating a letter to his secretary, Linda.

Dr. Terwin: "Dear Oliver: This is not the usual thank-you-for-the-referral note with the additional information that I have seen the patient and treatment has been arranged. You will know very well, dear Oliver, that things are somewhat different. My feelings are different, my expectations are different—so this letter will be different, too. It is more like a letter one writes before boarding a ship for an adventurous exploration of the unknown—a farewell letter. Big words! They may seem out of proportion to the unspectacular occasion. What, after all, is the big issue? An attempt at therapy under unusual circumstances? But every patient is unusual. There is always the risk, there is always a lot of unknown factors. Maybe it is the starting with a lie? Yet I shouldn't be too impressed by this bit of initial play-acting. I guess it is rather the challenge which goes with your expression of confidence! I have made an appointment with Porfiri for this afternoon, an hour from now. I liked his voice. I didn't find it difficult to talk to him—at least over the phone. But I still cannot imagine how it will go. I have a few sketchy ideas of what I am going to say. But I know that no preparation at all would be just as good—or better! Mrs. Porfiri referred to the inalienable privilege of the patient to say what he pleases. She is right; for a long time there will be no danger of arousing suspicion. The danger is rather of behaving too much like a patient. If for one reason or another the plan has to be abandoned or changed, I'll let you know! Wish me luck and thanks a lot! Yours. . . . " I would like to sign this letter before I leave and have it mailed before I come back.

Linda: O.K.

Dr. Terwin: I don't want to be tempted to add something after I meet Dr. Porfiri.

Linda: I see. You'll have it in a minute!

SCENE 3

Dr. Porfiri's office. Dr. Porfiri is sitting at his desk and talking into the telephone.

Dr. Porfiri: Sorry, I have to stop. I'm just about to see a new patient and I'm already late. 'Bye, Bob! *[He puts the receiver down, slumps somewhat in his chair, and sighs. Then he looks at his desk, begins straightening out the things on its surface, interrupts himself, gets up, and wanders about the room, like someone who is trying to bring about order but is not attentive to what he is doing. Finally he pulls himself together and goes over to the door of the waiting room and opens it.]* Dr. Terwin?

Dr. Terwin [entering]: How do you do, Dr. Porfiri? Very glad to meet you.

Dr. Porfiri: How do you do, Dr. Terwin? It is certainly—well, will you sit down? *[He steers Dr. Terwin to the chair at the side of his desk, then sits down behind the desk and takes up a pen.]*

Dr. Terwin: Thank you very much for arranging a meeting so soon after my call! *[He stops somewhat abruptly and looks toward the window.]* Very nice view!

Dr. Porfiri: Thank you, quite pleasant! Did I understand correctly—you wanted to consult me?

Dr. Terwin: Yes! Yes, I mean I would like to ask for your professional help—for myself!

Dr. Porfiri [frowning]: May I ask what made you pick me?

Dr. Terwin: I am new here, as you probably know. I relied on the recommendation of an old teacher of mine. *[Dr. Porfiri looks questioningly at him.]* Dr. Oliver Redstone. He was your teacher too, I understood, though this must have been some years before my time.

Dr. Porfiri: 1937 to '39.

Dr. Terwin: Well, I met him for the first time in—I think '42. *[Pause]* I have been in treatment once, during my training. I thought then that I did it in the first place for learning purposes. I now see it differently. Anyway, I thought I should be used to it by now, but I find myself quite uncomfortable when it comes to discussing my troubles. Mind if I smoke? *[Before Dr. Porfiri can answer, Dr. Terwin pulls out a package of cigarettes and lights one. Then he offers Dr. Porfiri the package.]*

Dr. Porfiri: No thanks! When did you start this treatment?

Dr. Terwin: During my residency—I think in '43.

Dr. Porfiri: And how long did it last?

Dr. Terwin: Close to three years, I guess.

Dr. Porfiri: Why was it terminated?

Dr. Terwin: Let's say mutual agreement. There were some improvements.

Dr. Porfiri: Improvements? In what?

Dr. Terwin: In what? A good question, Dr. Porfiri. I suppose in my symptoms. I—I had felt all kinds of anxieties, and after three years I felt them less, or less frequently, or I felt more ashamed to mention them. You see, I was then an advanced patient and a budding psychiatrist and—and felt under a kind of obligation to respond to treatment properly—that is, with improvement.

Dr. Porfiri: I see! And now?

Dr. Terwin [more seriously]: Now? Now I feel less obligated, or I have lost my power of imagination, my talent for self-deception. In a word, it doesn't work any more! *[Pause]* You probably are going to ask me what my symptoms are at the present time. You know, I often wonder to what degree the symptoms we hear so much about in our initial interviews are really the things our patients are bothered with most. In a way, I feel tempted to enumerate a whole lot of complaints, just because they have names. It is easy to say: I am suffering from insomnia of medium severity. Or to say: When I have to meet new people, I try to delay it, I feel an aversion to talking to them. I have to force myself into a conversation and usually fall silent after a short while.

I don't work as persistently as I would like and frequently I waste time. Or, I am irritable with my wife and my children. And so on and so forth. All that would be true. All these things bother me—occasionally—I could even say frequently. And yet—I wonder whether these and, maybe, a dozen similar complaints have made me come and look for help. *[He pauses and looks at Dr. Porfiri in a kind of impersonal evaluation, and then his glance goes toward the window and his face takes on an expression of absent-mindedness.]*

Dr. Porfiri [after having waited for a minute or so]: What, then, made you come?

Dr. Terwin: What made me come? Perhaps the fact that two obsessional thoughts creep into my mind every so often. Sometimes they both appear together. The one runs: ". . . and so it will go on forever and ever! How awful!" And the other goes: "Somewhere, at some moment, it will stop and it will be as if there never was anything, as if nothing ever had happened." And that is just as terrible!

Dr. Porfiri: Would you say that these thoughts are—at least sometimes—concomitant with experiences of depersonalization?

Dr. Terwin: I think you understand what I mean. "Concomitant with experiences of depersonalization," very good! I would venture to say that these thoughts or feelings *are* experiences of depersonalization.

Dr. Porfiri: Hm, I see. Can you say anything as to the time when these obsessive thoughts, to use your expression, first appeared or reappeared—or, maybe I should say, when they became so obnoxious that you started to think of—of consulting somebody?

Dr. Terwin: A year before we moved here we lost a child, my oldest daughter. She was 12 and died of a congenital heart disease. The long drawn-out alternation of hope and despair which preceded the final event was hard on all of us and left my wife, after all was over, in a state of depression or exhaustion, which was very disquieting. So, after four or five months had gone by without any noticeable change, I thought that it might help to change our surroundings. It took some time to make the decision and another six months before we actually moved. Well, as far as I can see, it really helped. From the moment the decision was made and the preparations started, there was a marked change for the better. Well, to answer your question: During the time when the decision to move had been made, but the move itself had not taken place, it occurred to me for the first time that it might be sensible for me to go into therapy again.

Dr. Porfiri: Can you say that at the time you thought of returning into therapy your wife's condition had already improved?

Dr. Terwin: I am not too sure, but it could be.

Dr. Porfiri: The illness and death of your oldest daughter must have been a highly traumatic experience, not only for your wife, but also for yourself. And yet you seem in no way to connect your symptomatology with these tragic events.

Dr. Terwin [after a short pause]: I do not feel any connection.

Dr. Porfiri: That's what I assume. But isn't it astonishing that you did not even *think* of a connection?

Dr. Terwin: There aren't so many things left that I can find truly astonishing!

Dr. Porfiri: You told me that your wife felt better after the decision to move, and I take it that she has improved even more since the move, but you—you seem to feel worse here than in the other city, don't you?

Dr. Terwin: I have no way to tell, except that here I am arranging for treatment while there I managed without. But that doesn't prove anything. *[Pause]* By the way, when could you take me? Once I made this decision. . . . *[He finishes the sentence by a silent gesture.]*

Dr. Porfiri: Well, as a matter of fact—I have hours open; you could start any time.

Dr. Terwin: Very good! If it's O.K. with you I'll come twice a week. As to the hours, the later in the day the better.

Dr. Porfiri: How about Monday and Friday at 7 P.M.?

Dr. Terwin: Friday is fine; could we make it Tuesday instead of Monday?

Dr. Porfiri: I guess that will be possible. I'll find out, before our next meeting.

Dr. Terwin: Oh—well—what is your fee?

Dr. Porfiri: Twenty dollars the hour.

Dr. Terwin: All right; so I'll see you. . . .

Dr. Porfiri: There is plenty of time left. I am free until 6. If you want to start right now?

Dr. Terwin [after a short hesitation]: All right.

Dr. Porfiri: Let's sit over there! *[They move to other chairs.]*

Dr. Terwin: It sounds ridiculous, but I feel as if I had really done something—spectacular!

Dr. Porfiri: Well, you made a decision.

Dr. Terwin: No, my mind was made up before I came that I would give it a try anyway. *[Pause]*

Dr. Porfiri: I know so little about you yet. Won't you tell me something about your background, your upbringing, and so on?

Dr. Terwin [a bit sadly]: Come down to business? So that work can start? Is that what you mean?

Dr. Porfiri [with friendly reproach]: Of course, you know as well as I that I need a lot of information!

Dr. Terwin: Be it as you wish! I am 42 now. Of my parents I remember only my father. My mother died when I was 2 years old. I have a picture of her in my mind, but when I describe it to my sister she says it's all wrong. As she is eight years my senior she must be right, and I must have confused our mother with some other female . . .

SCENE 4

Dr. Terwin's office. Linda is sorting some papers.

Dr. Terwin [entering from the hall]: Hello, Linda!

Linda: Hello, Dr. Terwin! Back already? Cured?

Dr. Terwin: Almost, almost, Linda—of my megalomania. What I let myself in for! Likeable person, Dr. Porfiri, very likeable. But I feel lost. You can't make a plan. I mean, I made a plan; but I couldn't stick to it. At the end I felt very exhausted. Not that it had been difficult to talk, on the contrary! I would never have thought before that it could be that attractive to the patient! This inalienable right to say what one pleases!

Linda: What, then, was so exhausting? Did you have difficulty in sounding convincing?

Dr. Terwin: As a matter of fact, I was not concerned with sounding convincing. The thought never entered my mind. It rather took an effort to keep alert to the purpose of my visit.

Linda: You know, you sound quite excited!

Dr. Terwin: It is exciting and—confusing; and very different from what I expected.

Linda: Did the lying bother you much?

Dr. Terwin: I am ashamed to admit that no, it didn't; certainly not much. Once or twice, when I had to invent a bit in answering a direct question, I felt some pangs. But otherwise—no! I must be more used to it than I thought. But, then, there weren't so many lies required. Since the other guy assumes that you are coming for treatment, every little idea that goes beyond "Hello" and "How are you?" will appear to him as a symptom. When I come to think of it—I was more truthful in this one hour than any member of the faculty ever is in any staff conference, myself included. You know: the patient's inalienable right. It includes —strange as it may sound—the right to say the truth.

Linda: I knew it! It mustn't be bad at all to be a patient! What would you think of extending this right to other people too—let's say, to secretaries?

Dr. Terwin: God forbid! What a subversive idea!

SCENE 5

Dr. Porfiri's office. Dr. Porfiri is talking through the half-open door to a patient who is just leaving.

Dr. Porfiri: We'll talk about that day after tomorrow—at 10 A.M. Good-bye!

Woman's voice: Tell me only one thing: You really think that I wanted to hurt him?

Dr. Porfiri [against his will]: I can't know what you wanted. *I* did not say that you wanted to hurt him—only *you* said so!

Woman's voice: But Dr. Porfiri, you know very well that I can't really know. *You* have to tell me!

Dr. Porfiri [pained and without a smile]: But not before day after tomorrow at 10 A.M. Good-bye!

Woman's voice: You are cruel! *[The door is slammed shut.] Dr. Porfiri almost falls into his chair, drops his arms lifelessly, and lowers his head until his chin touches his chest.*

Dr. Porfiri [murmuring]: In a way she is right—she is damned right! *He sits motionless, staring at the floor. There is a knock at the door. Startled, he jumps up and for a moment faces the door, uncertain what to do. Another knock makes him unlock the door carefully and open it a bit. He says:* Oh, it's you! Come in, quick! *[Mrs. Porfiri enters.]*

Dr. Porfiri: I am sorry. I have hardly any time. What is it?

Mrs. Porfiri: Hi, Emilio! I was just at Cynthia's. Her husband, Phil, came home early and we thought it would be nice if the four of us could eat out together. So I ran over to ask you—I thought you had this hour free—would you like to come?

Dr. Porfiri: Too bad! I can't. The hour has been filled again. You're quite right, it has been free. But now it isn't.

Mrs. Porfiri: Can't you skip it?

Dr. Porfiri: No, the patient must be already here, and besides, he's a new patient and a colleague to boot.

Mrs. Porfiri: What a pity! Maybe you can cut the hour short?

Dr. Porfiri: I tell you, I'd like to! The man is a nightmare!

Mrs. Porfiri: So sick, you mean?

Dr. Porfiri: No, not sick, but he's a queer guy, with a very evasive way of talking. It's hard to understand what he's really talking about.

Mrs. Porfiri: Confused?

Dr. Porfiri: No, not confused. He is very bright and yet—sort of unpredictable, I would say. Why don't you go on with Cynthia and Phil and I'll see you later at home. *[Points toward the waiting room.]* He, too, is a student of Oliver's!

Mrs. Porfiri: Really? No, I'll be at home and have dinner with you. We can dine with the Tenners another time! All right? I'm off! *[She leaves.]*

Dr. Porfiri: O.K. *[He sighs. Then he walks slowly toward the waiting room door, looking around as if he were searching for a way out. Finally he shrugs his shoulders and opens the door.]* Hello, Dr. Terwin!

Dr. Terwin: Hello, Dr. Porfiri! *[They sit down in chairs facing each other. There is a pause, during which Dr. Terwin carefully studies him vis-à-vis.]* You look brave. I like brave people. But I don't like to be the one to provide them with an opportunity to prove their courage. *[He pauses a little, so as to give Dr. Porfiri a chance to answer.]* But, as it is, that can't be helped, can it?

Dr. Porfiri: I am not sure that I understand you. You feel irritated?

Dr. Terwin: Not irritated, Dr. Porfiri! No, not irritated! But I notice that you don't seem especially happy to see me!

Dr. Porfiri [with a smile]: You expect people to feel happy whenever you appear?

Dr. Terwin: Of course not! I confess I was somewhat facetious when I said that you did not seem especially happy to see me. I meant only that you had a somewhat strained expression on your face, as if—as if you had to brace yourself—you know, a long working day and now, at 7 P.M., one more patient.

Dr. Porfiri: You might be right!

Dr. Terwin: Of course, I don't expect people to be happy just to see me. But maybe it would be nice if it happened—let's say—occasionally. *[Pause]* I am tired too. It seemed a very long day to me. There were not only the patients. I had to talk at a meeting—a group of social workers—quite interesting, but it's difficult for me to see their problems clearly. So it was strenuous. When I feel tired, I tend to become philosophical. I wonder whether other people react in the same way. As long as I am alert and wide awake I enjoy the details, like to see and to listen, to observe, I might say. But when I feel fatigued, I think in generalities, of generalities, and everything takes on a philosophical color. It becomes confused and self-contradictory—which is so characteristic of philosophical thoughts. No, no—I don't want to say anything against philosophy! We cannot skip over confusion. It seems an important ingredient of our thinking and its development. What is clear from the beginning isn't worth much.

Dr. Porfiri: If your theory is correct, you must be very tired indeed, as you are becoming more philosophical by the minute. But I don't think that your philosophical bent is the effect of fatigue. It rather serves a purpose. It helps you evade the real issue.

Dr. Terwin: The real issue? What's that?

Dr. Porfiri [seriously and somewhat sadly]: I can hardly believe that you don't know what I mean. I mean, of course, the things you want help for! Your philosophical speculations about the worthlessness of statements that are perfectly clear from the beginning might be very true, but in terms of your therapy—as you know as well as I—to dwell on such thoughts is simply a waste of time.

Dr. Terwin [after some hesitation]: A waste of time! As a matter of fact, I don't know as well as you. I have my doubts there. But be that as it may! You know, I made a discovery, or should I say a rediscovery? I even talked to my secretary about it. Linda is her name. She is a very sensible person—originally a social worker but—one of the exceptions. You know, I would say that it belongs to those features of her that constitute her exceptionality that she had no qualms about becoming a secretary instead of continuing to do social work. Well, my rediscovery! I say *re*discovery because I assume I must have discovered this trivial truth in my first treatment with Ingelman. Yet I can't say that I remember doing so, as this whole treatment has almost completely faded from my memory. Even the name of my therapist has only now come back—Ingelman! I am sure that if you had asked me in the previous hour who my therapist was, I would not have been able to conjure up the name. What I wanted to say is that after our previous hour, I realized what a great thing we offer our patients—*that they may say whatever they want to.* Even if we set aside the question of final results and whether we really help them or not, this opportunity to talk—to talk about what you feel like talking about—is unique. However little our patients may avail themselves of this marvelous chance, it is the most humane feature of therapy. You must think differently; or, at least, when you think of results and achievements, you feel that enjoying this unique opportunity to the fullest is a waste of time, or could possibly be a waste of time. And, as a conscientious therapist myself, somehow I have got the notion that you are a very conscientious therapist—you don't want your patient to waste time. Your brows contract a little, almost to the point of a frown. It is as if you had heard the call of duty, and, your face looking strained and somewhat sad, you dismiss humanity with a shrug and offer the warning: "You are wasting time!" *[Pause]* I admit that I respect this conscientiousness of yours—it has dignity. It certainly has. But, since it makes you look sad, it makes me feel sad too. I don't know how I would feel if you were not saddened by your submission to duty but pronounced your warning with a ringing voice and a sparkle in your eye. Maybe I would feel annoyed! Maybe I would laugh. As it is—and I can almost hear you sigh, figuratively speaking—well, here again the thought is creeping up: This will go on and on forever and ever. How awful!

Dr. Porfiri: This?

Dr. Terwin: What I mean by "this"? I'll tell you. Look how many things we have in common. We are approximately the same age and of a very similar background. We have gotten our training, partially at least, in the same place with the same teacher. We are both psychiatrists in private practice, doing psychotherapy essentially and by choice. As I did not know you before I made our first appointment, I would not have come without Oliver Redstone's mediation. But I would not have arranged for further visits, after our first interview, if I had not felt—well, that I could talk to you. Well, all these conditions making for ready mutual understanding being fulfilled in our case, all comes to naught because of the preoccupation with purpose, with rules and regulations, with wasting time and good use of time, with theory and psychological concepts—in one word, with duty!

Dr. Porfiri [after a pause of a minute]: You sound so—well, should I say enthusiastic—almost passionate. And yet, would you ever say such things to a patient of yours?

Dr. Terwin: Do you want me to talk to you as if you were my patient?

Dr. Porfiri: Of course not! But you can't have one truth for your patients and another one for yourself!

Dr. Terwin: True, very true—and I don't!

Dr. Porfiri: You know, it seems that you have an aversion to seeing yourself in the role of a patient.

Dr. Terwin: That's very true. I have an aversion to seeing myself in any kind of role. That is essentially what I said before, though in different words. *[There is a pause of more than a minute, and then he continues in a low voice.]* I even find it unsatisfactory to see others acting a role.

Dr. Porfiri: I am not sure that I understand you.

Dr. Terwin: Perhaps you understand but don't like to think you do?

Dr. Porfiri [after a moment's hesitation]: I think that is correct. I, somehow, feel that you are critical of me, but I can't put my finger on it. When I listen to you, there are moments when I feel I understand what you mean and in a way, could agree. But then, a few seconds later, I have lost you, and I get confused.

Dr. Terwin [after 30 seconds]: You see, Dr. Porfiri, I feel much better now. It is, of course, not a law of nature, or of logic or anything like that. There certainly are exceptions, but by and large I think it is true that if things are clear from the beginning, the exchange is not worthwhile. Only the transition from misunderstanding and confusion to—maybe only a faint sense of approaching a vague notion of something that was possibly meant. Well, it is completely empirical, but I have come to distrust a conversation where everything is lucid and transparent and one says, "Yes, indeed," or "No, under no conditions."

Well, as I said, there are probably exceptions. I am not impatient. I don't have to have everything at once. And I don't expect others to expect that either. Isn't that what our job consists of most of the time, and especially where it is not in vain? Well, we use up a lot of time—we deal with months and years. We are very generous in this respect. And it would not make sense to be impatient. I often think that time has a different significance or, maybe, a different texture, in our job from what it has in many others. Though we are paid by the hour, our achievements do not consist of just surviving or staying awake for a certain number of minutes, as it is with the night watchman. Nor do we work like the pieceworker, who wants to cram into a given time as many holes drilled or springs soldered or bolts riveted as possible. One could say that we are not fighting time, neither urging it on to pass quicker, nor trying to slow it down and make it hold more. If everything goes well—whatever that means—we are at peace with time.

Dr. Porfiri [with some irritation in his voice]: You say "we"!

Dr. Terwin: Well, I assume that others might see it the same way I do.

Dr. Porfiri [with a wry expression on his face]: Or should see it the same way you do? Isn't that what you want to say?

Dr. Terwin [calmly]: Of course, I really meant to say something about the nature of our job that—more or less—everybody must notice.

Dr. Porfiri: And if they don't. . . .

Dr. Terwin: Oh, you disagree?

Dr. Porfiri: I did not say that!

Dr. Terwin: But you mean just that! *[Dr. Porfiri keeps silent, although it takes some effort. After more than a minute Dr. Terwin continues.]* So why shouldn't you disagree? Heavens, it wouldn't be the first time that two therapists disagree in how they view their work! I can't see anything bad about that. Do you?

Dr. Porfiri [with noticeable irritation, although he tries to keep calm]: It seems to me you constantly manage to ignore the fact that you come to me for treatment as a patient and not for a social visit as a colleague!

Dr. Terwin: And you feel that that is wrong. Well, there you may be right. And yet—I get confused. I may see things in the wrong perspective. But don't you expect that something must be wrong with a man who comes to see you for treatment? If he were not inclined to see himself or the other guy in a somewhat distorted way, what would be there for you to treat?

Dr. Porfiri: Aren't you playing with words?

Dr. Terwin: Good—that you say that! I guess I am. I know that I am tempted to do that very, very frequently. But when I do it, I don't recognize, or don't *always* recognize, that I am doing it. And sometimes—you see—sometimes I feel—Oh, my God, how can I say it and make myself understood? I feel that I am playing with words and at the same time—or by this very thing—but how could you possibly understand me? Well, perhaps I can say it this way: Sometimes—oh, not always, but sometimes—I can't find any better expression for what I want to say than just to play with words. It is like a curse! You'll probably call it an obsession! It *is* an obsession. It makes me sad or even desperate—I mean, trying to find the right words and not finding them, and playing with words instead. I get my thoughts entangled in sentences—and they are all in knots. It's like having a long wet fishing line that is all muddled up. You can't leave it alone, but the more you try to straighten it out, the more it gets entangled. So I can't leave it alone, can't stop talking and allow things to settle themselves. I have to talk on and add words, and more and more and more words, and it goes on and on and looks like an aimless playing and leads to nothing—most of the time. And there again I have the feeling: This will go on and on forever and ever. How awful!

Dr. Porfiri: Well, I think we better stop here. The time is not quite up—but I am tired, I must say—it would not . . .

Dr. Terwin: Oh, that is all right! We don't have to be pedantic. I am tired myself. I'll see you—?

Dr. Porfiri: Tuesday—same hour.

Dr. Terwin: Good-bye!

Dr. Porfiri: Good-bye, Dr. Terwin! *[He does not look up when Dr. Terwin leaves. He appears disconcerted, brooding, and agitated at the same time.]* Thank goodness! It's over—finally. *[He sits down and looks very dejected. Two minutes pass. The telephone rings.]* Hello! Estella! Yes, I will. I can do that—easily. No, nothing special—tired perhaps. Yes, indeed. I don't know what Oliver had in mind. He didn't care to send me a note. So I don't know what he thinks about his protégé—or what he knows of him, for that matter. But I will write him. It is really a kind of imposition. Crazy! Yes, I said crazy and I mean it—very obscure—can't make him out. It is really very inconsiderate of Redstone—maybe it is old age! Practically no excuse—no, no—well intentioned, sure—but there is only a limited amount of good intentions one can survive—yes, I'll have to write him anyway! No, I won't forget. I'll leave soon! See you! *[He puts the receiver down with a sigh.]*

SCENE 6

Dr. Terwin's office, about two weeks later. Linda is working at her desk. The telephone rings. Linda is visibly reluctant to take off the receiver, but when it rings for the fourth time she can't hold out.

Linda: Dr. Terwin's office! No, not yet, Madam . . . I don't know. You called earlier? It's all right, but. . . . No, no. . . . Perhaps you can try later in the afternoon. Do you want to leave a message? Well, as you prefer. . . . *[Puts down the receiver.]* That's she!

[Dr. Terwin enters. He looks tired and preoccupied.]

Dr. Terwin: I am late, I know. I should really refuse to take part in these conferences. There's no point in it—formalities—*[Looks at her for the first time.]* Eh—what's the matter, Linda, you look so gloomy? *[As she says nothing but seems to be searching for words, he becomes alarmed.]* Has something gone wrong? What is it? Speak up! Dr. Porfiri—?

Linda: I am afraid that something is wrong! Mrs. Porfiri called—I don't know how many times. She didn't give her name, but I recognized her voice. She may call again any minute.

Dr. Terwin [frowning]: Well, hm, that's just too bad; I can't talk to her. But, you know, she has been under stress now for a long time. Besides, I am seeing Dr. Porfiri tonight. Today is Friday, isn't it? *[Linda nods].* O.K.—so I will see him. What more can I do? *[He sits down. The telephone rings.]*

Linda [agitatedly]: If it's she, I think you should talk to her! Dr. Porfiri wants to stop! *[The telephone rings again.]*

Dr. Terwin: What's that? Answer the phone and tell her that I'm not in yet but will be in 15 minutes.

Linda [desperately]: You have a message from Dr. Redstone about Dr. Porfiri! *[The telephone rings.]*

Dr. Terwin [firmly]: Take it and tell her what I told you to!

Linda [into the phone]: Hello, Dr. Terwin's office! Beg pardon? Whom did you say? No, you've got the wrong number! We are not the dry cleaners!

Dr. Terwin: Heaven knows what we are! What was that about Dr. Porfiri's stopping? Did he cancel tonight's hour?

Linda: I should have told you first! *[She is trying to control her voice.]*

Dr. Terwin [his hands on his forehead]: My God, already! It would have been the seventh hour—three weeks! When did he call?

Linda: He didn't! You got me wrong. There was a message from Dr. Redstone. . . .

Dr. Terwin: From Dr. Redstone? *[He takes the receiver off the telephone and puts it on the table.]* I want to get this straight! Not from Dr. Porfiri but from Dr. Redstone?

Linda: I am sorry; a night letter came this morning from Dr. Redstone. Here it is!

Dr. Terwin [reading]: "Decided to let you know. Disturbed letter from Emilio. Accuses me of not telling him in advance about you. Calls you evasive, unpredictable, conceited, crazy, hostile. Without transition says all his own fault. Apologizes, thanks for my damnable, misplaced confidence. Estella called me, desperate about Emilio's getting worse, talking daily about that 'new patient.' Wants to terminate. I am ready to take next plane if you think advisable. Sorry, Oliver." Hm, that's it?

Linda [almost in tears]: Oh, Dr. Terwin, I knew the odds were all against you. But I had wished so much you would succeed. *[She takes the receiver to put it back on the phone.]*

Dr. Terwin: Wait, leave it on the table; let's have it nice and quiet—for a while at least! We'll do some thinking! The night letter was sent last night. Since mail reaches Oliver's mountain retreat only once a day, at 10 in the morning, Emilio's letter must have gotten there yesterday—Thursday morning. An airmail letter takes three full days to get from here to Oliver's wilderness, so Emilio's disturbed message can't have been mailed any later than Monday morning. That fits nicely with the mood of the letter. This type of confused message one may write late at night after a miserable weekend.

Linda: But what's your point?

Dr. Terwin: Now look! I saw Dr. Porfiri in my Tuesday evening hour! Well, whatever he may have felt or thought—and at times he became quite emotional—he neither looked nor acted like one who is about to withdraw! And this was two days after he wrote the alarming letter, two days in which he had time to plan appropriate action. So he *gets* irritated and furious and *says* alarming things to poor Mrs. Estella. What, really, could we expect? If what I am doing with him is therapy at all, it must have the effect of therapy whether he thinks of it as therapy or as a course in Esperanto! And the effect of therapy is what it always is and should be: It stirs him up, tempts him to step out of his rut; and when he does and feels the wind blowing and in his first bewilderment and panic tries to bury himself even deeper—well, that's what every patient does when therapy takes. Now, with Dr. Porfiri things have to go at a sharper pace; they simply have to.

Linda: At a sharper pace?

Dr. Terwin: If any other patient under the influence of treatment steps out of his rut and then, frightened, runs for shelter again, he can soften the impact of therapy for a while by blaming the therapist and fighting him. But Dr. Porfiri can't fight his therapist because, so far as he knows, this man is his patient, with whom he should not get involved in a fight. Here his professional self-esteem is at stake.

Linda [still shaky]: I am glad you see it that way, and I can understand what you meant by a sharper pace. But how can you know that this extraordinary dilemma he is in will not lead to a disastrous explosion?

Dr. Terwin: I don't know. Or rather, I know it must lead to an explosion. This situation cannot last long. The question is only: Will the little breeze of fresh air that made him unbutton his neurotic straitjacket be sufficient to make him accept normal treatment?

Linda: I see; but how can one take this risk?

Dr. Terwin: Only if one realizes that one would take an equal or even worse risk by refusing to risk, if you see what I mean.

Linda [thoughtfully]: I do.

Dr. Terwin: I have to leave for my hour! Put the receiver back and send a wire to Oliver: "Don't see advisability of visit. Tonight's appointment still uncanceled. Don't see danger increased. Love, Simon." I'm off!

Linda: Good luck! *[Dr. Terwin leaves.]* What a life!

SCENE 7

Dr. Porfiri's office. Dr. Terwin is sitting in the patient's chair, while Dr. Porfiri is talking over the phone.

Dr. Porfiri [into the phone]: No, I can't. I will call you back at, let's see—8 sharp. *[He puts the receiver down and addresses Dr. Terwin.]* Sorry, I interrupted you!

Dr. Terwin: Did you? I can't remember having said anything. As far as I am concerned, you could have continued on the phone for the whole hour. I wasn't sure for a while whether I would come today or not. Isn't that ridiculous? When I ask myself what makes me reluctant to come here, I find that it's stage fright. Will I know my lines? Or more precisely: How can I make you listen? And I resent the effort.

Dr. Porfiri: You have the feeling that I don't listen to you?

Dr. Terwin: That's the trouble. You don't! You are so busy trying to find something you can do for me that you have no time, or rather no attention, left to listen.

Dr. Porfiri [fairly unperturbed]: This impression of yours that I do not listen carefully enough to what you are saying—don't you think that this is just a reflection of your own evasiveness, a projection, to use the proper word?

Dr. Terwin [after a glance at his opponent]: My evasiveness?

Dr. Porfiri: You—well, sometimes you talk about yourself; yet most of the time you talk about me or what I am doing with you!

Dr. Terwin: When you are at the dentist's and you say to him, "You are hurting me," are you talking about the dentist or are you talking about yourself? See what I mean? Someone might say: "I am afraid to drive home now in the rush hour," or "The show last night was superb," or "It's too bad you don't listen to me!" If you are primarily impressed by the grammar, you may say that the one who confesses fear of driving talks about himself, but the one who praises the show talks about the show, and I—when I complain that frequently you don't listen to me—I am talking about you. But all three of us are saying what it is that concerns us—right now, at the moment.

Dr. Porfiri [slightly uneasy, but forcing himself to speak in a serious, matter-of-fact tone]: I think I see what you mean. Your little lecture on the ambiguity of language or grammar might be perfectly correct. Yet the fact remains that you prefer to give a little lecture, which has nothing to do with the purpose of our sessions, instead of talking about your personal problems. *[With a smile which is meant to be friendly but comes out sarcastic]:* I am sure if one of your patients talked to you the way you did just now, you would describe him as an intellectualizer.

Dr. Terwin [thoughtfully]: The purpose of our sessions—look, if I were talking to you, for whatever purpose, and I saw you suddenly turn white and shiver and slump in your chair, would you expect me to continue talking about, let's say, the nomination of Dr. X for president of our psychiatric association, or about my insomnia, or about whatever we had planned to discuss? I would jump up and ask, "What is the matter with you?" and, perhaps, take your pulse; and it would be ridiculous to do otherwise—to pursue my topic in the very moment you are fainting.

Dr. Porfiri [with some sharpness]: Look, Dr. Terwin, look at your parallel! That's what you are fantasying about and wishing for: namely, that I fall ill right here under your nose and you jump up and take my pulse and act as the doctor and turn me into the patient. You are fighting your role as a patient and want to reverse the positions!

Dr. Terwin: I think you have a point there, Dr. Porfiri—although, perhaps, not exactly the point you want to make. Let me say first that I don't think that I would feel any satisfaction if you fainted or suffered any kind of physical accident. It would embarrass me terribly. I am not good at physical medicine and never was. I would call the nearest GP and would be afraid I might have failed to apply the proper first-aid measure. So I don't think that I wish you to fall ill. But you perceived something that I too recognize as true. It is—no, let me say it in this way: I am not sure that I would notice it if you were only to change color. But I do notice it when you are not listening to me. And it's more than just noticing it. It jolts me and absorbs my attention. If it happens it is for me: the business at hand, the one I want to attend to. Well, you see, here I think you made a good point. This sensitivity—or call it hypersensitivity if you want to—I developed in working as a therapist, or maybe it determined my becoming a therapist.

Dr. Porfiri [puzzled]: This sensitivity?

Dr. Terwin: Well, the fact that it pains me if the other person is not listening to my words but is only registering them, as it were—that he does not talk to me but only exposes me to information, if I may say so.

Dr. Porfiri [incredulously]: And that, you say, determined your becoming a therapist?

Dr. Terwin: I feel it is the essence of my being a therapist! Therefore, although I can't quite go along with your formulation, I would say you made a good point when you complained that I don't adhere to my role as a patient. As a matter of fact, I don't know what the role of the patient is. Are there things that only the therapist should say and other things reserved for the patient? From my viewpoint, that is not so! You are quite right when you assume that frequently the things I am saying to you I could also have said to a patient of mine, and vice versa. Well, the expression "vice versa" is not clear. What I mean is: Sometimes patients say things to me that I could have said to them or to other patients. For instance, it has happened that a patient has said to me: "You are not listening to me!"

Dr. Porfiri [spontaneously, and regretting it later]: And how did you react then?

Dr. Terwin [with a light smile]: Of course, not always in the same way, but sometimes I have seen that the patient was right. In one case, I remember, I had noticed the patient's beautiful tie and suddenly thought of a suit of mine, which I needed for that very evening but had forgotten to fetch from the cleaners. So . . .

Dr. Porfiri [interrupting almost against his will]: And what do you think is preventing me from listening to you?

Dr. Terwin: I might say: your preoccupation with therapy!

Dr. Porfiri: My what?

Dr. Terwin [calmly]: Your preoccupation with therapy. What I mean is: You are obviously under the urge to do something—oh—therapeutic!—no matter what you feel or how you feel. You are keeping yourself, should I say, protected, or at a distance from what I am saying, so that you can manage not to take it in, not as you would take in an ordinary telephone message or the question of your neighbor when he asks you whether your electricity has been cut off too, or something like that. I am sure, for instance, that in this very moment you are uneasy about whether you are doing right to be interested in my views on therapy, or rather, to permit yourself to act upon this interest and ask questions about them, instead of looking into the significance of my talking the way I do, interpreting it, using it as sample behavior as a psychologist uses the Rorschach responses of his subject.

Dr. Porfiri [jumps up from his chair, paces around his desk and, with an effort, sits down again]: Excuse me—Why are you talking to me in this way? No, that's not what I wanted to say! Sorry! *[He makes several attempts to say something, but unsuccessfully.]*

Dr. Terwin [seriously]: Are you sure? I rather got the impression that that was exactly what you felt like saying, while at the same time you seemed to feel you shouldn't.

Dr. Porfiri [passionately]: You know damned well I shouldn't.

Dr. Terwin: Not at all! Look, Dr. Porfiri, I think—and I have no doubt you will agree with me—it is a sad truth that rarely, very, very rarely do people say what they feel like saying. Here we are, the both of us, in this office together, free for an hour to say what we think. We do not have to sell anything to each other, nor do we have to agree on bylaws or resolutions. We don't have to fight each other, beguile each other, persuade each other. we might not always grasp immediately the other's meaning, but we have the potential of doing so. Why waste this unique opportunity?

Dr. Porfiri [he now has one of his knees drawn up, the elbow of his right arm on the knee, and his forehead resting in his right hand. His searching glance, under drawn brows, is on Dr. Terwin's face, with an expression as if he were in a dream and trying to awake]: Whatever the merits or demerits of your reasoning, if I may call it that, it certainly has the effect of confusing me—surprisingly. No, that is not even the whole story. If you were only confusing me, it would not be so strange! There are many things so complicated, or complex, or maybe even paradoxical—one is uncertain about them, bewildered, and one needs time to get them organized. Nothing unusual about that. So what? I get confused, so I shut up and give myself time to think! But, look, what am I doing? [*With lowered voice*] I don't shut up, I continue talking—in spite of knowing better. I could say—I feel tempted to say: You are seducing me?! And so I say it! But what is the sense of putting the blame on you? You are the patient, or supposed to be the patient, so you have the privilege of talking seductive nonsense. But I, supposedly the therapist, should be able to stand up to it. I should be able to hold my own and not to succumb, no matter what you say. [*More firmly*] There is only one way out of this situation—and you know it!

Dr. Terwin: At least, I know what you mean. However, you seem to me like one who has been brought up in a religious faith, and then one day discovers that he does not believe in God. And he is terrified! "My God," It is true?! I can see it—you have violated your principles, but—does not what you would call the violation consist of doubting them?

Dr. Porfiri [again in a low voice]: My principles—?

Dr. Terwin: Well, the word is questionable. It might be more than mere principles. I think it is no accident that it occurs so rarely that people say what they mean.

Dr. Porfiri [with an effort, looking Dr. Terwin straight in the face]: I understand what you say, but I cannot help but feel that I should not, and that I would be better off if I didn't or couldn't! But not even that is completely true! Be that as it may—one thing is for sure! I cannot treat you!

Dr. Terwin: Be that as it may—it seems pretty immaterial in comparison with the fact that we—at least at times—have managed to say to each other what we meant! I—I think that I might do even slightly better the next time! I see there are only a few minutes left, and I would like to discuss this matter more fully. Would it be all right if I kept my next appointment—under whatever heading you wish?

Dr. Porfiri: Of course, Dr. Terwin, of course! I really should not—should not have . . .

Dr. Terwin: Don't worry! I feel fine! Day after tomorrow at 6—all right?

Dr. Porfiri [with a half smile]: All right!

INDEX

ABOUT THE AUTHOR

Louis B. Fierman, M.D., is a graduate of Case Western Reserve University School of Medicine. After completing a rotating internship at Cleveland Metropolitan General Hospital, he entered active duty in the army, and was assigned to Military Government in occupied Japan.

Returning to civilian life in the United States in 1949, Dr. Fierman entered residency training in internal medicine at Yale, switching to psychiatry with encouragement from his psychologist wife. He was appointed Chief Resident at both the Yale Psychiatric Institute and the Yale-New Haven Hospital Psychiatric Service and has remained on the clinical faculty of the Yale School of Medicine. He taught psychotherapy and entered personal analysis with Hellmuth Kaiser, a psychoanalyst who had broken with traditional and orthodox psychoanalysis to devise a new and more effective psychotherapy. After Kaiser's death in 1961, Dr. Fierman published an anthology of Kaiser's works in 1965.

Dr. Fierman has been President of the Connecticut Psychiatric Society, Chief of the Psychiatric Service at the West Haven Veterans Administration Medical Center, Medical Director of Elmcrest Psychiatric Institute, and is in private practice in New Haven as Medical Director of Psychotherapy Associates. He is a Life Fellow of the American Psychiatric Association.

Now semiretired, Dr. Fierman has returned to his childhood interest in classical music and plays the French horn in local symphony orchestras.